PIPE FITTINGS

NIPPLES

PIPE LENGTHS
UP TO 22 FT.

STRAIGHT
COUPLING

REDUCING
COUPLING

COUPLING

NUT

CAP

STRAIGHT
TEE

REDUCING
TEE

STREET
TEE

STRAIGHT
CROSS

REDUCING
CROSS

90° ELBOW

90° ELBOW

90°
ELBOW

45°
ELBOW

REDUCING
ELBOW

90° STREET
ELBOW

45° STREET
ELBOW

45°
Y-BEND

REDUCING TEE

REDUCER

UNION (3 PARTS)

PLUG

BUSHING

CAP

RETURN BEND

90°

45°

UNION ELBOWS

STREET

UNION TEES

PLUG

45° ELBOW

TEE

MEASURES OF CAPACITY

1 cup	=	8 fl oz
2 cups	=	1 pint
2 pints	=	1 quart
4 quarts	=	1 gallon
2 gallons	=	1 peck
4 pecks	=	1 bushel

STANDARD STEEL PIPE ((All Dimensions in inches)

Nominal Size	Outside Diameter	Inside Diameter	Nominal Size	Outside Diameter	Inside Diameter
⅛	0.405	0.269	1	1.315	1.049
¼	0.540	0.364	1¼	1.660	1.380
⅜	0.675	0.493	1½	1.900	1.610
½	0.840	0.622	2	2.375	2.067
¾	1.050	0.824	2½	2.875	2.469

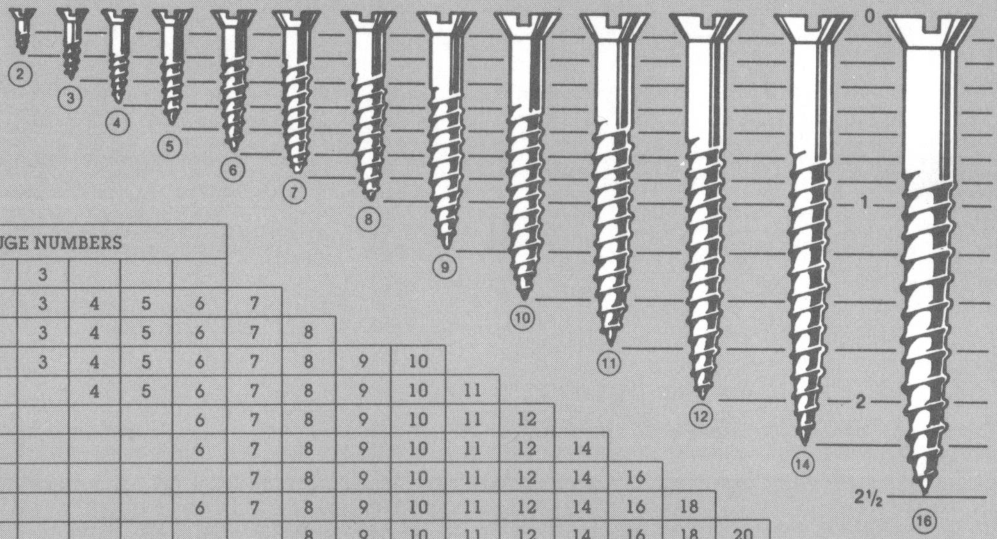

WOOD SCREWS

LENGTH	GAUGE NUMBERS												
¼ INCH	0	1	2	3									
⅜ INCH			2	3	4	5	6	7					
½ INCH			2	3	4	5	6	7	8				
⅝ INCH				3	4	5	6	7	8	9	10		
¾ INCH					4	5	6	7	8	9	10	11	
⅞ INCH							6	7	8	9	10	11	12
1 INCH							6	7	8	9	10	11	12	14
1¼ INCH								7	8	9	10	11	12	14	16
1½ INCH							6	7	8	9	10	11	12	14	16	18
1¾ INCH									8	9	10	11	12	14	16	18	20
2 INCH									8	9	10	11	12	14	16	18	20
2¼ INCH										9	10	11	12	14	16	18	20
2½ INCH													12	14	16	18	20
2¾ INCH														14	16	18	20
3 INCH															16	18	20
3½ INCH																18	20	24
4 INCH																18	20	24

WHEN YOU BUY SCREWS, SPECIFY (1) LENGTH, (2) GAUGE NUMBER, (3) TYPE OF HEAD—FLAT, ROUND, OR OVAL, (4) MATERIAL—STEEL, BRASS, BRONZE, ETC., (5) FINISH—BRIGHT, STEEL BLUED, CADMIUM, NICKEL, OR CHROMIUM PLATED.

Popular Mechanics

do-it-yourself encyclopedia

The complete, illustrated home reference guide from the world's most authoritative source for today's how-to-do-it information.

Volume 13

HOLIDAY PROJECTS

to

HOMES

HEARST DIRECT BOOKS

NEW YORK

Acknowledgements

The Popular Mechanics Encyclopedia is published with the consent and cooperation of POPULAR MECHANICS Magazine.

For POPULAR MECHANICS Magazine:

Editor-in-Chief: *Joe Oldham*
Managing Editor: *Bill Hartford*
Special Features Editor: *Sheldon M. Gallager*
Automotive Editor: *Wade A. Hoyt, SAE*
Home and Shop Editor: *Steve Willson*
Electronics Editor: *Stephen A. Booth*
Boating, Outdoors and Travel Editor: *Timothy H. Cole*
Science Editor: *Dennis Eskow*

Popular Mechanics Encyclopedia

Project Director: *Boyd Griffin*
Manufacturing: *Ron Schoenfeld*
Assistant Editors: *Cynthia W. Lockhart Peter McCann, Rosanna Petruccio*
Production Coordinator: *Peter McCann*

The staff of Popular Mechanics Encyclopedia is grateful to the following individuals and organizations:

Editor: *C. Edward Cavert*
Editor Emeritus: *Clifford B. Hicks*
Production: *Layla Productions*
Production Director: *Lori Stein*
Book Design: *The Bentwood Studio*
Art Director: *Jos. Trautwein*
Design Consultant: *Suzanne Bennett & Associates*
Illustrations: *AP Graphics, Evelyne Johnson Associates, Popular Mechanics Magazine, Vantage Art.*

Contributing Writers: Penelope Angell, *Christmas decorations for holiday cheer,* page 1540; Ivan Berger, *Burglar protection in your home,* page 1621; Rosario Capotosto, *Burglar-proof your house the low cost way,* page 1632; Richard F. Dempewolff, *Add on to your home and save,* page 1572; Mark Fineman, *Greeting cards from your photos,* page 1563; Rudolph F. Graf & George J. Whalen, *Your house number belongs in lights,* page 1611; Len Hilts, *How to spot a good house,* page 1653; Joh. H. Ingersoll, *Water in your basement— how to stop it,* page 1613; *Burglar alarm systems for your home,* page 1616; Mike McClintock, *Room addition planning,* page 1570; *Windows let the sun shine in,* page 1598; John Pearson and Harry Wicks, *Hide your valuables,* page 1638; Tim Snider, *Building codes,* page 1661; Stephen Walton, *Home improvement projects,* page 1581; William J. Ward, Jr., *What makes a good house plan?,* page 1640; Harry Wicks, *Enlarge and facelift your kitchen,* page 1602; *Save inside a Colonial cabinet,* page 1634; Steven Willson, *Wainscoting,* page 1607.

Picture Credits: Popular Mechanics Encyclopedia is grateful to the following for permission to reprint their photographs: Mr. Richard F. Dempewolff, page 1572; Home Planners, Inc., pages 1642-1652; United Gilsonite Laboratories, page 1653 (top).

ISBN 0-87851-166-0

Library of Congress 85-81760

10 9 8 7 6 5 4

PRINTED IN THE UNITED STATES OF AMERICA

Contents

Gifts to make for Christmas

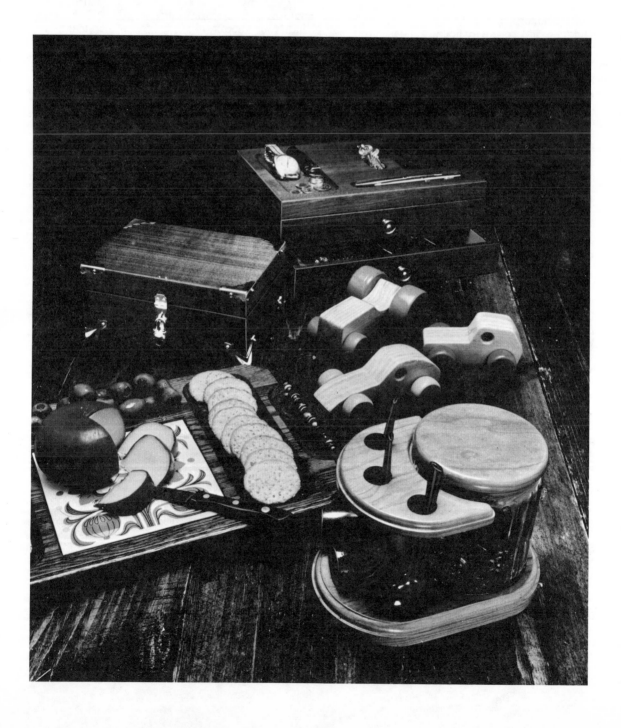

Treasure chest

IT'S LITTLE MORE than a plain wooden box, but add solid-brass hardware and a tiny padlock after giving it a hand-rubbed finish, and it takes on the look of a handsome miniature treasure chest. It's a gift most anyone can use to keep trinkets and other personal possessions under lock and key. Make it from pine or walnut, ¼ to ½ in. thick, and glue it together as a complete box. Sand it well and, with your table-saw blade projecting a bit more than the thickness of the wood, carefully saw around the four sides, as shown at the right, to form the lid. Some screws must be filed flush when the box is made of ¼-in. wood. Use brass hardware—two hinges, four corners, four feet, a hasp and padlock. Red velvet lining adds the finishing touch.

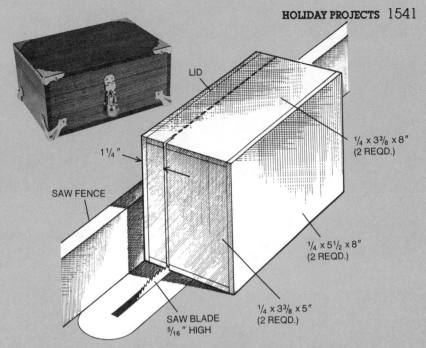

LID

1¼"

SAW FENCE

SAW BLADE
5/16" HIGH

¼ x 3⅜ x 8"
(2 REQD.)

¼ x 5½ x 8"
(2 REQD.)

¼ x 3⅜ x 5"
(2 REQD.)

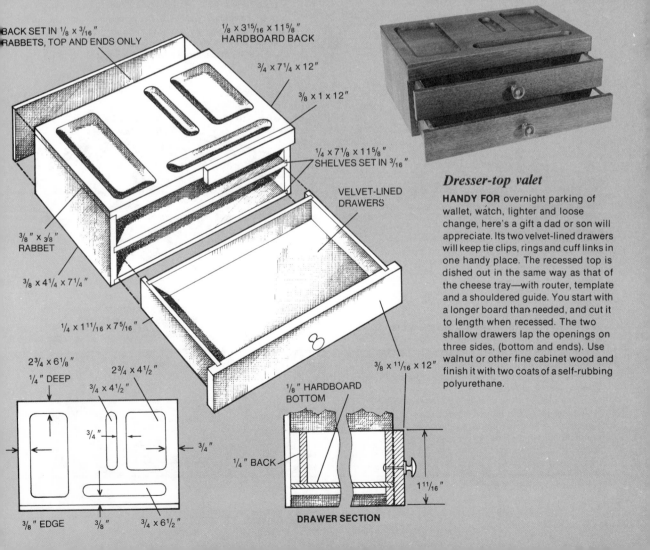

BACK SET IN ⅛ x 3/16"
RABBETS, TOP AND ENDS ONLY

⅛ x 3 15/16 x 11⅝"
HARDBOARD BACK

¾ x 7¼ x 12"

⅜ x 1 x 12"

¼ x 7⅛ x 11⅝"
SHELVES SET IN 3/16"

VELVET-LINED
DRAWERS

⅜" x ⅜"
RABBET

⅜ x 4¼ x 7¼"

¼ x 1 11/16 x 7 5/16"

2¾ x 6⅛"
¼" DEEP

2¾ x 4½"

¾ x 4½"

¾"

¾"

⅜" EDGE   ⅜"   ¾ x 6½"

⅛" HARDBOARD
BOTTOM

¼" BACK

1 11/16"

⅜ x 11/16 x 12"

DRAWER SECTION

Dresser-top valet

HANDY FOR overnight parking of wallet, watch, lighter and loose change, here's a gift a dad or son will appreciate. Its two velvet-lined drawers will keep tie clips, rings and cuff links in one handy place. The recessed top is dished out in the same way as that of the cheese tray—with router, template and a shouldered guide. You start with a longer board than needed, and cut it to length when recessed. The two shallow drawers lap the openings on three sides, (bottom and ends). Use walnut or other fine cabinet wood and finish it with two coats of a self-rubbing polyurethane.

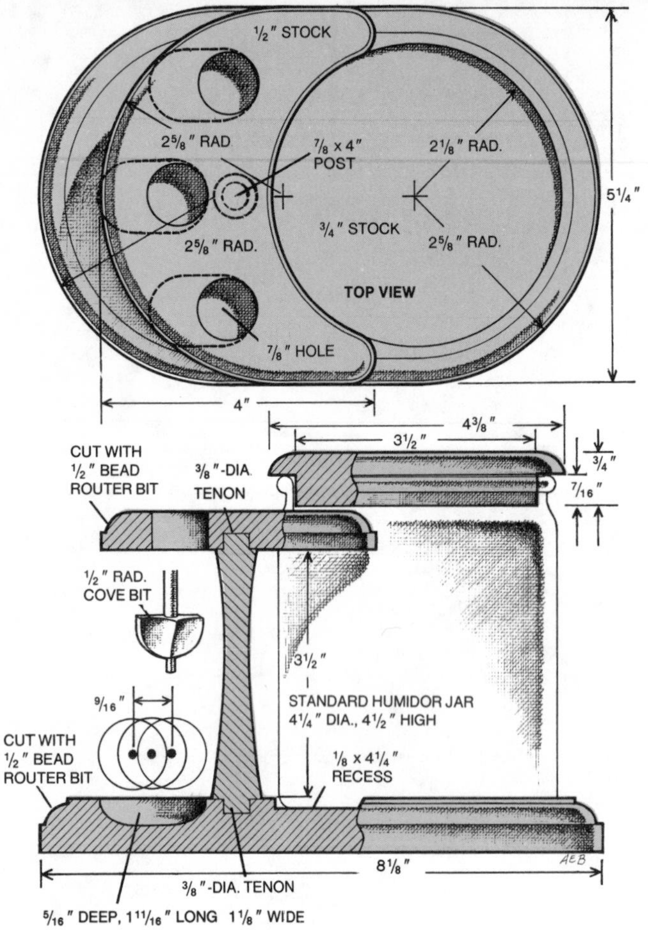
1/2″ STOCK
2 5/8″ RAD.
7/8 x 4″ POST
2 1/8″ RAD.
5 1/4″
3/4″ STOCK
2 5/8″ RAD.
2 5/8″ RAD.
TOP VIEW
7/8″ HOLE
4″
4 3/8″
3 1/2″
3/4″
7/16″
CUT WITH 1/2″ BEAD ROUTER BIT
3/8″-DIA. TENON
1/2″ RAD. COVE BIT
3 1/2″
9/16″
STANDARD HUMIDOR JAR 4 1/4″ DIA., 4 1/2″ HIGH
CUT WITH 1/2″ BEAD ROUTER BIT
1/8 x 4 1/4″ RECESS
8 1/8″
AEB
3/8″-DIA. TENON
5/16″ DEEP, 1 11/16″ LONG 1 1/8″ WIDE

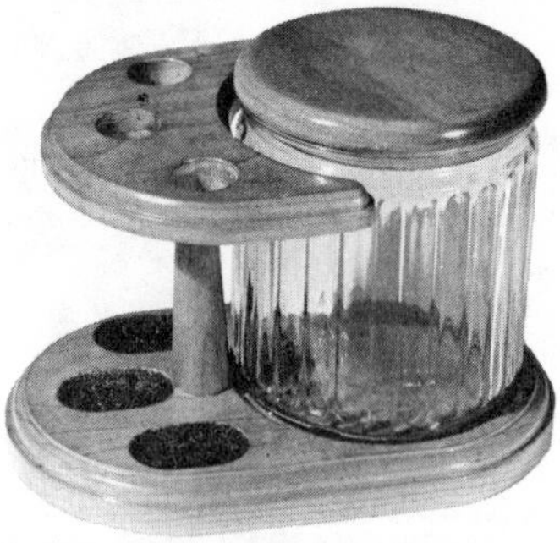

Pipe rack and humidor

A PIPE SMOKER'S DREAM, this pipe rack and humidor set makes a great gift for a pipe lover. It's a lathe, router and drill-press project holding three pipes and a tobacco jar you can buy at any pipe shop. The jar rests in a 1/8-in.-deep recess you make with a circle cutter, then a router and a straight bit. The three oval wells for pipe bowls are made with a 1/2-in.-radius cove router bit chucked in the drill press. The bit is guided by three holes the same size as its pilot and lowered 3/8 in. into the work. Overlapping depressions are evened up with a wood chisel and holes filled with wood putty. If you wish, you can line wells with modelmaker's grass sprinkled in wet glue. The jar cover is faceplate-turned to fit, and a spindle made to support the rack 3 1/2 in. above the pipe wells. Edges of rack and base are shaped with a 1/2-in.-bead bit. Green felt is glued to the bottom for a finishing touch.

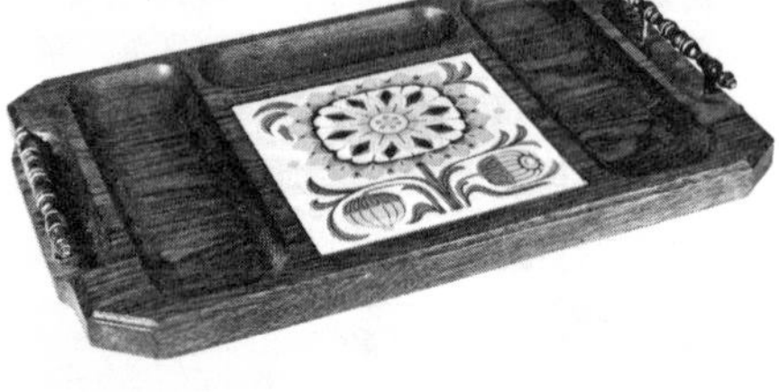

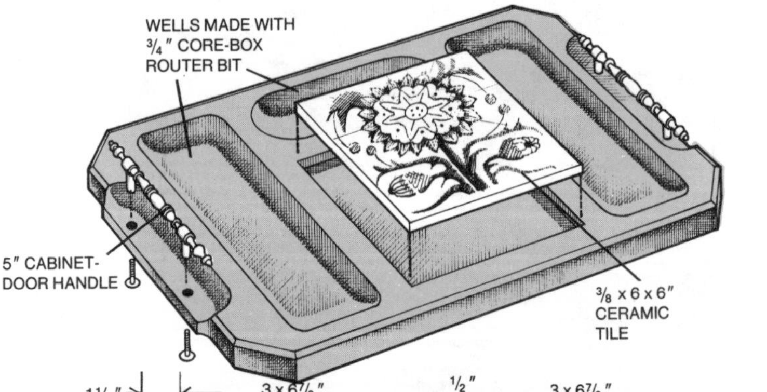
WELLS MADE WITH 3/4″ CORE-BOX ROUTER BIT
5″ CABINET-DOOR HANDLE
3/8 x 6 x 6″ CERAMIC TILE

Cheese tray

A DECORATIVE 6x6-in. ceramic tile is used for the cutting surface of this handsome cheese tray. The three olive and cracker depressions, and the tile recess, are made with a router and a hardboard template that's used to guide the cutter. Openings in the template are made 3/16 in. less all around than overall sizes of the recesses to accommodate a shouldered guide ring that fits the base of the router. Short brads driven through ends of template hold it in place. A 3/4-in.-dia. core-box cutter is used to scoop out the olive and cracker "trays" and a straight bit to cut the tile recess. Routed areas at handle ends of the tray are made last with the core-box bit.

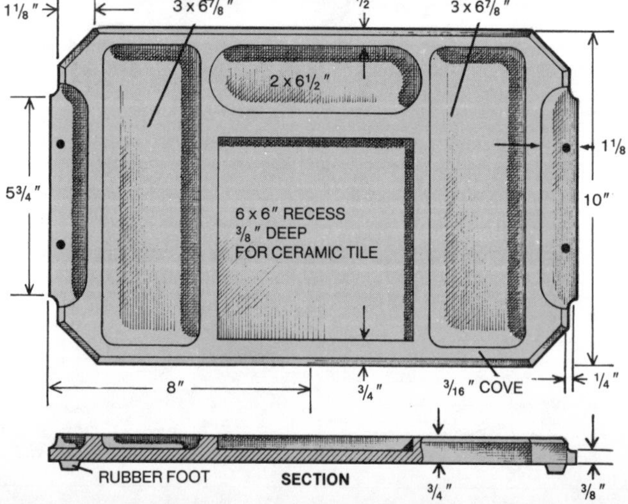
1 1/8″
3 x 6 7/8″
1/2″
3 x 6 7/8″
2 x 6 1/2″
1 1/8″
5 3/4″
10″
6 x 6″ RECESS 3/8″ DEEP FOR CERAMIC TILE
8″
3/4″
3/16″ COVE
1/4″
RUBBER FOOT
SECTION
3/4″
3/8″

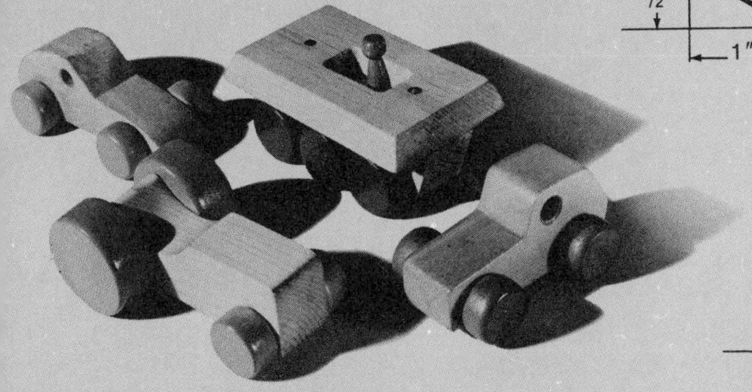

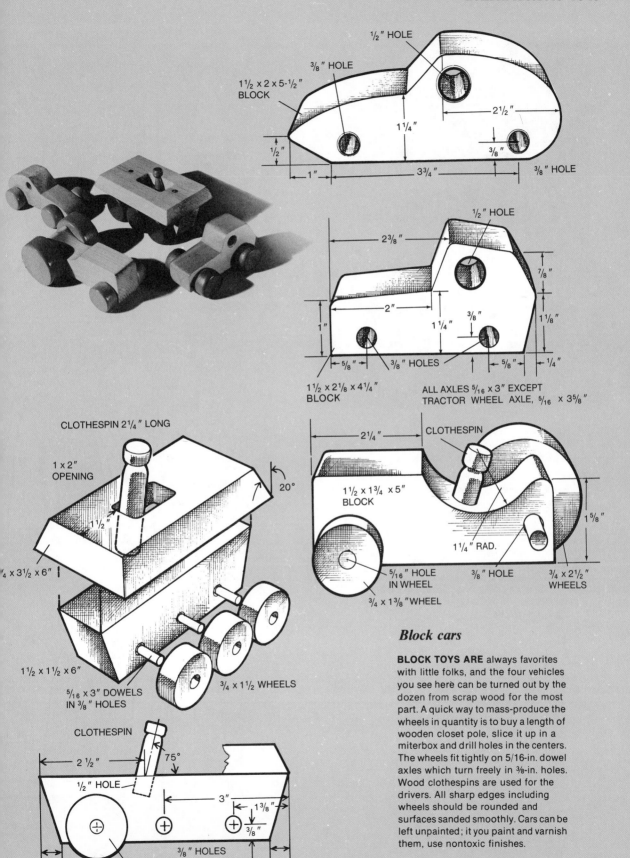

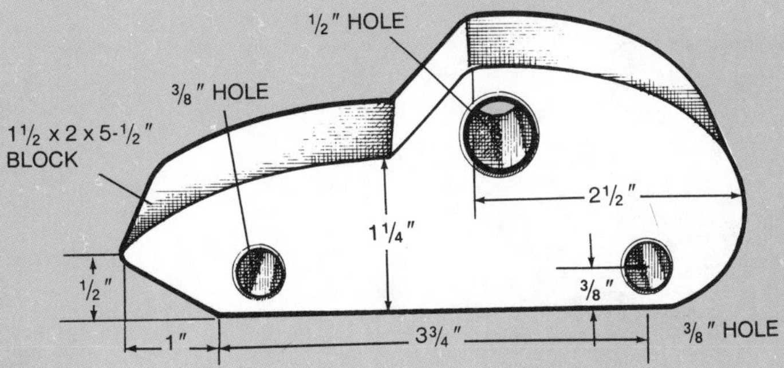
1/2″ HOLE
3/8″ HOLE
1 1/2 x 2 x 5-1/2″ BLOCK
2 1/2″
1 1/4″
1/2″
3/8″
1″
3 3/4″
3/8″ HOLE

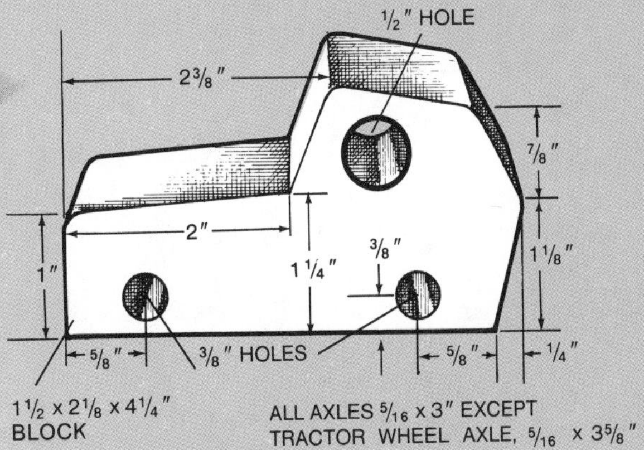
1/2″ HOLE
2 3/8″
7/8″
2″
1″
1 1/4″
3/8″
1 1/8″
5/8″
3/8″ HOLES
5/8″
1/4″
1 1/2 x 2 1/8 x 4 1/4″ BLOCK
ALL AXLES 5/16 x 3″ EXCEPT TRACTOR WHEEL AXLE, 5/16 x 3 5/8″

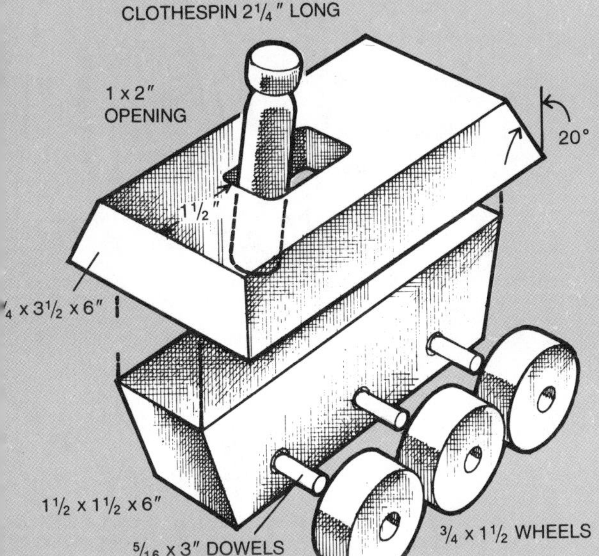
CLOTHESPIN 2 1/4″ LONG
1 x 2″ OPENING
20°
1 1/2″
/4 x 3 1/2 x 6″
1 1/2 x 1 1/2 x 6″
5/16 x 3″ DOWELS IN 3/8″ HOLES
3/4 x 1 1/2 WHEELS

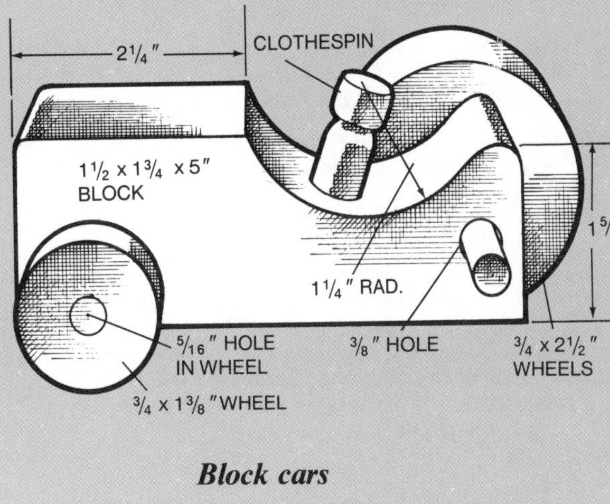
2 1/4″
CLOTHESPIN
1 1/2 x 1 3/4 x 5″ BLOCK
1 5/8″
1 1/4″ RAD.
5/16″ HOLE IN WHEEL
3/8″ HOLE
3/4 x 2 1/2″ WHEELS
3/4 x 1 3/8″ WHEEL

Block cars

BLOCK TOYS ARE always favorites with little folks, and the four vehicles you see here can be turned out by the dozen from scrap wood for the most part. A quick way to mass-produce the wheels in quantity is to buy a length of wooden closet pole, slice it up in a miterbox and drill holes in the centers. The wheels fit tightly on 5/16-in. dowel axles which turn freely in 3/8-in. holes. Wood clothespins are used for the drivers. All sharp edges including wheels should be rounded and surfaces sanded smoothly. Cars can be left unpainted; it you paint and varnish them, use nontoxic finishes.

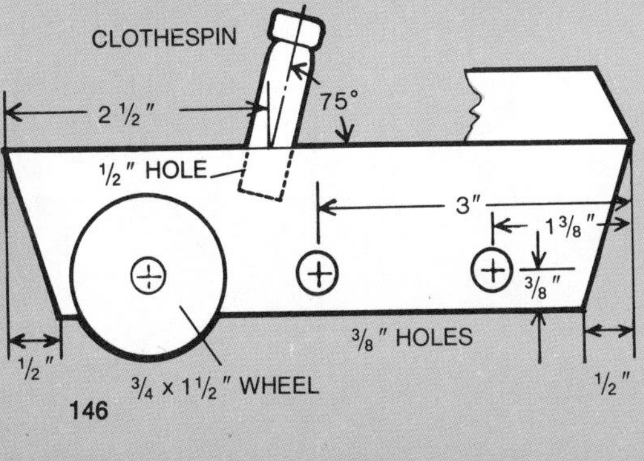
CLOTHESPIN
2 1/2″
75°
1/2″ HOLE
3″
1 3/8″
3/8″
3/8″ HOLES
1/2″
3/4 x 1 1/2″ WHEEL
1/2″

Artisan's musical crèche

THIS CLASSIC Nativity scene takes on an unusual and thoroughly modern look when imaginatively made as an abstract.

Both the figures and the shelter require some hand carving to bring out some of the finer details but a beginner's talent here lends a realistic and authentic touch. As detailed in the patterns at right, the lathe-turned figures are quite presentable without the carving, however, should you so desire.

Another option is the inclusion of a music works that fits neatly in the small boxlike structure on the right of the crèche.

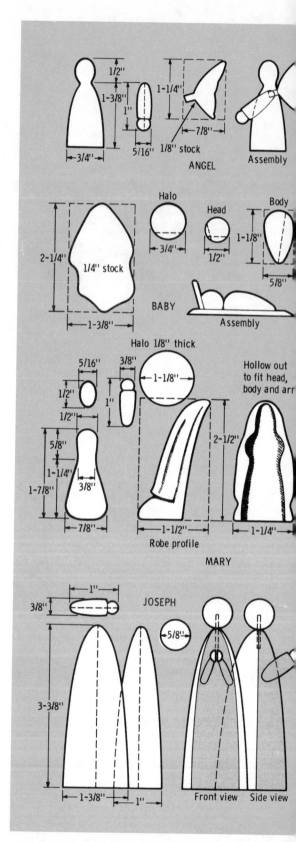

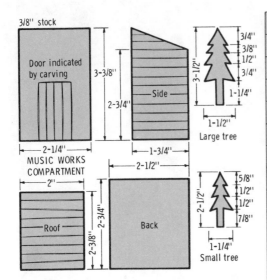

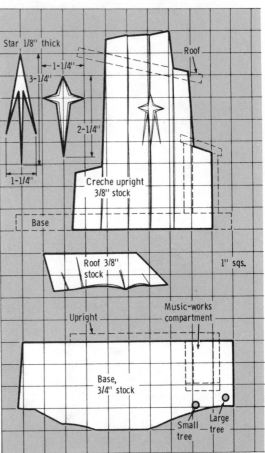

FIGURES ARE made up of different wood species as listed, then finished to suit your preference (below left). Trees (below right) also need some rough carving.

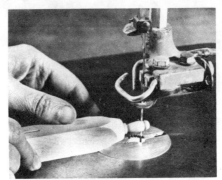

COMPACT MUSIC movement fits tidily into neat structure on right side of crèche. Jigsaw is required as is some carving (left).

Greeting cards from your photos

WOULD YOU LIKE to send a truly unique card this year? Greeting cards which incorporate photographs are certainly that, and with a bit of care can be quite professional looking as well.

If making your own cards seems like too big a project to tackle, many commercial processors and photo and department stores offer services which combine your favorite prints or slides with a standardized holiday message. Most of the commercially composed cards are in color and vary in price from about 25 cents to 50 cents per card, depending upon their complexity. But cards you print yourself will undoubtedly cost less, and they can be made for all occasions.

Start with a good negative—one that requires no specialized printing techniques such as burning-in or dodging. Such tricks are too much trouble when you have to turn out cards by the dozen. The picture should have good contrast and be sharp, too.

Pick your envelopes as soon as you decide what type of card you want to make, since the envelope controls the size of the finished product. Most stationers stock envelopes in many different sizes and colors, but that won't help you if you've printed up a batch of cards for which no suitable envelopes are available. (Of course, you could always make your own envelopes, or design a self-mailing card with a flap that folds over to protect the picture and to carry the stamps and mailing address.)

One of the simplest cards consists of a

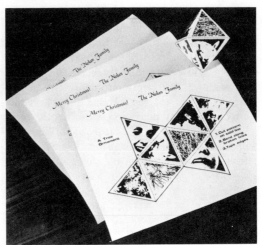

THIS PERSONALIZED tree ornament is made from one high-contrast negative combining greetings, directions on how to cut and fold, and eight triangular photos.

photograph mounted on a piece of cardboard with space for a handwritten greeting or message. Mounting can be a problem, however. Dry-mounting tissue is best, but it's also time-con-

BLACK-AND-WHITE cards are easy to make at home. For details on how these were made, see the text and photos.

suming and requires a dry-mounting press for best results. Kodak mounting cement or 3M spray-mounting adhesive will work reasonably well but may present difficulties if the prints are wrinkled. Even plain old rubber cement can be used; with this the print may separate from the board over time and the solvents may effect the clarity of the print, but if you know that the card will only be viewed for a short period of time (no more than a month or two), rubber cement may be your best bet. It's easy, it's cheap, and excess amounts can be rubbed off with the tip of a finger.

Art supply stores carry an array of mounting boards, and an ordinary card can be transformed into a dazzler by picking the right color or texture for the surrounding mount board. Silver matte board, which lends a rich elegant tone to even otherwise commonplace black-and-white photographs, is especially effective.

Some card designs require tricky darkroom work; but if you're not adept at this, or lack time, you can take a lot of short-cuts with your camera. A time-honored way is to combine members of your family and their greeting in one shot by posing them with a letter sign bearing the proper message or with a symbolic prop, such as a Christmas tree.

A contact sheet of negatives from a roll of 120 film can make a new and interesting greeting card idea. A sequence of family poses can be

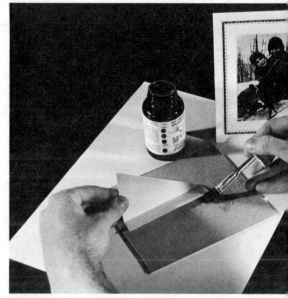

ADDING A SIMPLE EASEL BACK turns flat prints into stand-up keepsakes. The easel can be oriented for either horizontal or vertical photographs.

exposed on the entire 12-exposure roll to give your relatives and friends a kaleidoscopic view of your family. When printing the contact sheet, leave one frame blank to insert your greeting and have a place to sign the card.

With some careful planning the contact-sheet

COMBINING GREETINGS AND PHOTO on one negative for easy, one-step printing takes time in the beginning, saves it in the end. Here, greetings are lettered with Prestype onto high-contrast print; reshooting on high-contrast film results in a negative (right) from which you can make as many prints as you like.

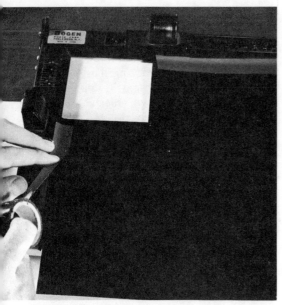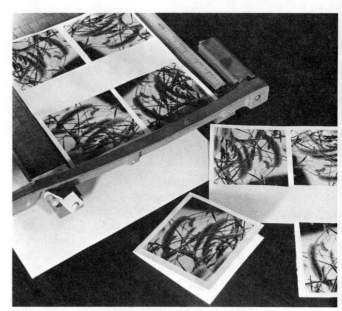

FOR EASY MULTIPLE PRINTING, mask off all but one corner of your photo easel with opaque cardboard (left) so that the cardboard swings up with the easel's masking frame. Insert paper for the first exposure, then turn it 90° for each of three additional exposures. Now you can process the four prints as one, cutting them apart (right) once they've dried.

method also can be used to make several cards at once. By repeating the same sequence of pictures three or four times, a single proof sheet of 120 film will yield several multiple-picture "cards" which can be mounted or sent as-is, a considerable saving in darkroom time. And since this type of card doesn't require an enlarger, it's ideal for those just getting started in darkroom work.

You can also put four *enlargements* on a single sheet of paper. It saves surprising amounts of time and aggravation: no more cutting paper in the dim illumination of a safelight, no more shuffling tiny chips of paper through the developer, stop-bath and fixer—instead, you just process one nice, big 8x10 for each four prints, then cut them apart in full room light when they're washed and dry.

Here's how: Make a simple mask by cutting a 3½-inch square from one corner of an 11-inch square of heavy cardboard. Adjust the easel's masking bands (if it has them) for a 3½-inch square print, then tape the mask to the easel's hinged upper masking frame with black tape. Insert the 8x10 paper, make the first exposure,

then rotate the paper 90° for the second exposure. Continue, rotating after each exposure, until all four corners have been exposed. Then process the sheet and cut apart the individual prints to mount on your cards.

When you plan on making many prints from a normal or high-contrast copy negative, you can often save time by shooting several paste-ups at once onto a single copy negative. That way a single print will yield several cards in one operation—all you have to do is trim them apart afterward.

Some interesting cards combine photographic and nonphotographic ideas. The tree ornament, a form of folded sculpture, is one example. It is a flat pattern which can be folded and taped into a solid. Each of the triangular areas that become the sides of the finished polygon are filled with photos that work well in high contrast, and both greetings and assembly instructions are added in Prestype on the portions of the card outside the pattern area. Then the resulting paste-up is shot on high-contrast film. The end product is a most unusual holiday greeting, one that will stand out among the deluge of commercial cards.

Musical centerpieces

■ YOU CAN MAKE this Christmas a truly musical one by using your cassette tape recorder to provide personalized "built-in" sound in your table centerpieces. The three examples shown are designed so that any cassette recorder may be slipped in place, from the side or bottom.

The tunnel-like candelabra consists of 13 layers which stand like slices of bread. Except for the center layer, there are two each of identical overall size and shape. Both ends are alike also, ex-cept that the removable one has a centering plug glued to its back.

Since two pairs of each layer are alike, the U-shaped sides are bandsawed four at a time. This is done by first stacking the ¾ x 1½-in. pieces (all cut to proper length) in a block and holding them together with masking tape. As there is only one "A" layer, only two pieces would be stacked for cutting.

The U-shaped pieces are joined together at top and bottom with identical-length cross pieces. All are ⅝-in. wide so that when they are glued to the ¾-in. side pieces, ⅛-in. slots remain between the individual layers.

When all layers are completed they're glued together and clamped into a single block, taking care to keep all even at the sides. "Stringing" them on a scrap board will help to keep them aligned.

The Styrofoam tree has a base made up of five plywood discs, the bottom one being removable for placing a recorder inside. Sound comes out through a perforated metal band wrapped

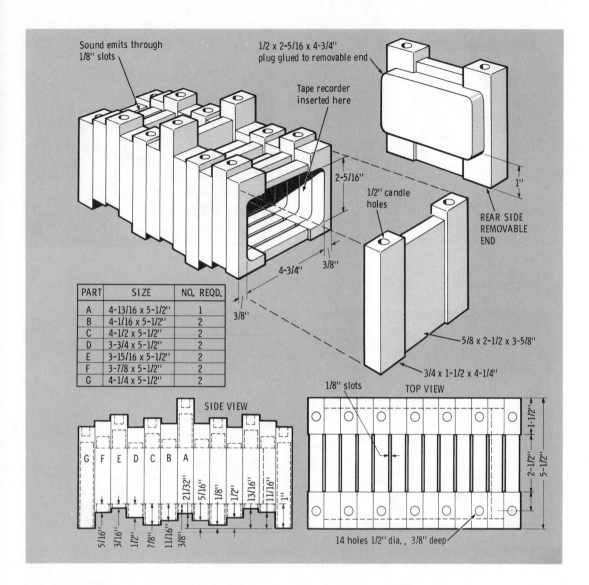

Sound emits through 1/8" slots

1/2 x 2-5/16 x 4-3/4" plug glued to removable end

Tape recorder inserted here

2-5/16"

1/2" candle holes

REAR SIDE REMOVABLE END

1"

4-3/4" 3/8"

5/8 x 2-1/2 x 3-5/8"

3/4 x 1-1/2 x 4-1/4"

3/8"

PART	SIZE	NO. REQD.
A	4-13/16 x 5-1/2"	1
B	4-1/16 x 5-1/2"	2
C	4-1/2 x 5-1/2"	2
D	3-3/4 x 5-1/2"	2
E	3-15/16 x 5-1/2"	2
F	3-7/8 x 5-1/2"	2
G	4-1/4 x 5-1/2"	2

SIDE VIEW

G F E D C B A

21/32" 5/16" 1/8" 1/2" 13/16" 11/16" 1"

5/16" 3/16" 1/2" 7/8" 11/16" 3/8"

1/8" slots   TOP VIEW

1-1/2" 2-1/2" 5-1/2"

14 holes 1/2" dia., 3/8" deep

around two discs that are made slightly smaller in diameter than the top and bottom ones to which they are glued. The different size creates rabbets for the metal band. The base is completed by gluing and nailing ¼-in. thick wooden fins completely around the circumference.

The tree itself is formed in a triangular hollow pyramid from 101 Styrofoam balls tack-glued together with an electric glue gun. Building them up is tricky but can be done with help by assembling each side flat on a table and then tacking the three sides together on the inside with glue. The completed tree should measure nine balls on a side, nine balls high.

The modern tree stand has an access door on one side. The details show how it's made of two six-sided discs cut from ¾-in. wood and then joined with five beveled side members to form a hexagonal drum. Prior to assembly ⅛-in. saw kerfs, radiating to the six corners, are made in the top and down the edges. The side members are actually lined up with the corner slots so you have a continuous ⅛-in. slot from top to bottom. The sixth side member is the door. This piece and the two adjacent to it have holes drilled in it to let the sound out.

The assembly is supported by six L-shape legs cut from tempered hardboard. These, as well as the narrow strips for the top, are inserted in the slots during final assembly. Note that the legs also fit in slots cut in a slotted central base block, which is glued to the bottom.

The base is covered with six pieces of bright red felt, starting from the 2-in. hole in the top and

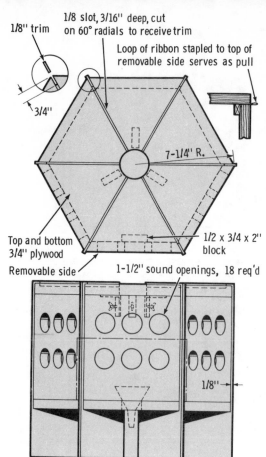

1/8" trim

1/8 slot, 3/16" deep, cut on 60° radials to receive trim

Loop of ribbon stapled to top of removable side serves as pull

3/4"

7-1/4" R.

Top and bottom 3/4" plywood

Removable side

1/2 x 3/4 x 2" block

1-1/2" sound openings, 18 req'd

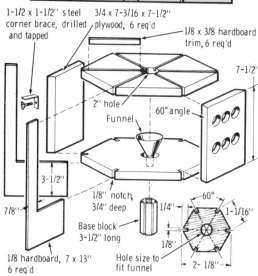

1/8"

HANDIEST WAY to assemble the Styrofoam balls is to tack-glue them with an electric glue gun.

1-1/2 x 1-1/2" steel corner brace, drilled and tapped

3/4 x 7-3/16 x 7-1/2" plywood, 6 req'd

1/8 x 3/8 hardboard trim, 6 req'd

7-1/2"

2" hole

Funnel

60° angle

3-1/2"

1/8" notch, 3/4" deep

7/8"

Base block 3-1/2" long

1/4"

60°

1-1/16"

1/8"

1/8 hardboard, 7 x 13" 6 req'd

Hole size to fit funnel

2- 1/8"

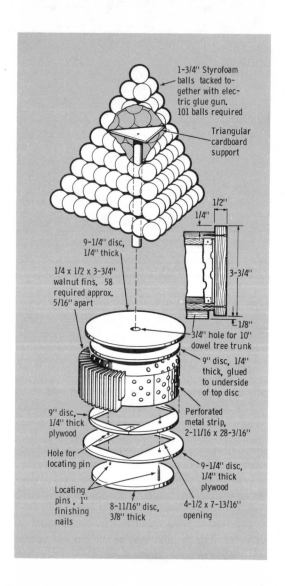

1-3/4" Styrofoam balls tacked to-gether with elec-tric glue gun. 101 balls required

Triangular cardboard support

9-1/4" disc, 1/4" thick

1/4 x 1/2 x 3-3/4" walnut fins. 58 required approx. 5/16" apart

1/2"

1/4"

3-3/4"

1/8"

3/4" hole for 10" dowel tree trunk

9" disc, 1/4" thick, glued to underside of top disc

9" disc, 1/4" thick plywood

Hole for locating pin

Perforated metal strip, 2-11/16 x 28-3/16"

9-1/4" disc, 1/4" thick plywood

Locating pins, 1" finishing nails

8-11/16" disc, 3/8" thick

4-1/2 x 7-13/16" opening

bringing it down the side. These are cut to lap the slots slightly and are stapled at the hole and to the underside of the base. The hardboard legs and the narrow top strips hold the felt in the slots. In the case of the door opening the felt is tacked to the underside of the top. The door is covered separately with enough felt being left at the bottom to provide for tacking it to the under-side of the base. This provides a hinge.

Christmas decorations for holiday cheer

■ THE REAL JOY AND CELEBRATION of the holiday season can be the months of planning that precede it. Craftsmen and designers have come up with some beautiful decoration projects for your holidays. A few hours in your workshop will make sure your home will look its festive best during the holidays.

General painting directions

You can achieve a high-gloss look on painted wood projects with this technique:

Sand the project smooth by starting with 120-grit paper. Use 180-grit paper to finish. Dust the piece and wipe it with a tack cloth.

A fast, efficient way to seal small pieces is to use an acrylic spray. You might consider the alternative of using a mixture of equal parts 3-lb. cut white shellac and denatured alcohol. Rub lightly with 220-grit sandpaper, dust, and wipe with a tack cloth.

Apply a prime coat of white spray primer or the primer made by the maker of the finish-coat

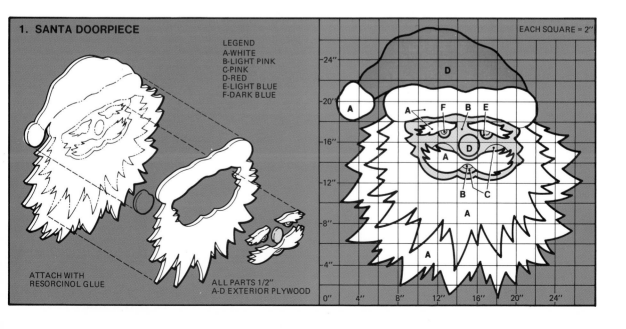

1. SANTA DOORPIECE

LEGEND
A-WHITE
B-LIGHT PINK
C-PINK
D-RED
E-LIGHT BLUE
F-DARK BLUE

ATTACH WITH RESORCINOL GLUE

ALL PARTS 1/2" A-D EXTERIOR PLYWOOD

EACH SQUARE = 2"

enamel you plan to apply. Lightly sand with 220-grit paper, and dust and wipe with a tack cloth. Finally, spray on a coat of enamel; let it dry, sand lightly with 240-grit paper, dust, wipe with a tack cloth, and spray on a final enamel coat.

1 Santa doorpiece

Layered pieces of plywood give this doorpiece a pleasing dimensional effect.

> Materials: 1 piece A-D exterior plywood, ½x26x48 in.; wood plastic filler; pigmented shellac; denatured alcohol; plastic or exterior enamel paints in the following colors: white, red, pink, dark blue; sawtooth wall hanger; resorcinol glue; sandpaper; medium and small paintbrushes as needed.

1. Make a grid on the plywood and draw pieces to size; see plan.

2. Cut out all parts with a scroll or sabre saw. Fill all edge voids with wood plastic filler. Sand with 120-grit abrasive, wipe with a tack cloth.

3. Seal, apply pigmented shellac undercoat as outlined in general painting directions.

4. Using the photo as a guide, apply red and white paints. Also mix white and pink to make light pink and paint that area. Add white to dark blue and paint eyes. Let dry.

5. Next, paint pink cheeks, dark blue area of eyes and pink part of mouth. Let dry.

6. Glue parts, clamp and let dry overnight.

7. Install sawtooth wall hanger on back, making sure that it is centered. Hang by suspending from nail or picture hanger.

2 Gingerbread ornament

These gingerbread ornaments are simple projects that children will enjoy decorating.

> Materials: 1 piece hardboard, ⅛x4½x5 in. for each ornament; 2 oz. bottles of Sobo glue (1 for each color of frosting); flour; liquid food color; white acrylic paint; skewer or stir stick; straight pin; cord for hangers; clear acrylic spray coating.

1. Make full-size patterns for the gingerbread ornaments; see plan.

2. Transfer the patterns to the hardboard. Either draw around a cardboard pattern or use some carbon paper to trace a paper pattern.

3. Cut out the shapes using a sabre or jigsaw with a fine blade and a slow feed rate. When cutting toward narrow or pointed areas (i.e.; under arms), cut both lines toward the point and drop out waste.

4. To make the icing, remove about one tablespoon of glue from the bottle. Remove the nozzle cap and pour enough flour into the bottle to thicken the glue, keeping it so it can still be squeezed through the nozzle cap. Stir well with the skewer. Stir white acrylic paint into the mixture. (Use a squib about ¾-in. long if squeezed from a pigment tube.) If a color other than white is wanted, add drops of food color until desired tint is obtained. Mixture will dry slightly darker than it appears wet. Mix *very* well. Replace nozzle cap. Mix other colors as needed.

5. Practice a few lines and dots on scrap until you gain control; then decorate the ornaments. There will be air bubbles if the glue is recently

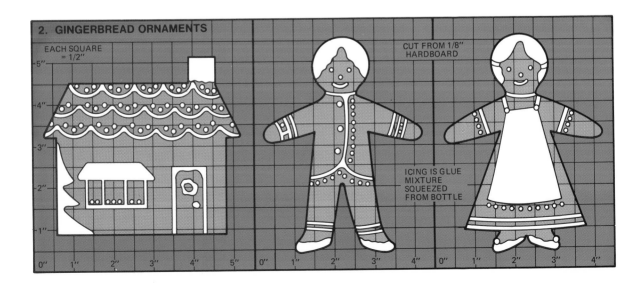

2. GINGERBREAD ORNAMENTS

EACH SQUARE = 1/2"

CUT FROM 1/8" HARDBOARD

ICING IS GLUE MIXTURE SQUEEZED FROM BOTTLE

mixed. These can be pricked with a pin. To avoid color bleed when two colors of icing touch, allow one to form a skin before applying the second color. Let dry.

6. Spray completely with a clear coating.

7. Decorate the back side of the hardboard.

8. Make a cord loop, trimming ends near the loop. Glue knot to top of ornament.

3 Candle pot centerpiece

The flower-pot candle holder is a spectacular centerpiece when filled with Christmas balls and tapers or multicolored candles of varying sizes. Sheets of color dye paper to make the designs are available in a kit.

> Materials: 1 9-in. top dia. clay flower pot; 1 piece heavy white fabric scrap, 2½x33 in.; 1 8-in. dia. wood disc (false bottom); 1 tube acrylic paint in red or other bright color; foliage; contact cement; heavy-duty aluminum foil to cover wood disc; candle holders and candles as wanted.

1. Color the flower pot with acrylic paint.

2. Cut a wood disc to make a false bottom.

3. Gather ferns, small leaves or other pleasingly shaped foliage. Flatten and dry it by sandwiching between pages of a newspaper and ironing with a hot iron.

4. Remove the top page of the newspaper and position a sheet of color dye paper face down over the leaf. Apply iron to transfer dye to the leaf.

5. To transfer the dye on the leaf to the rim fabric, place the leaf, colored side down, on the fabric. Cover with protective paper and apply heat. Continue flattening and dying foliage and then transferring color to the rim fabric as you desire.

6. Cement fabric to the pot.

7. Cover wood disc with aluminum foil and insert in pot.

3

8. Arrange Christmas balls and candles in holders in the pot.

4 Train garland

You can make the train garland as short or as long as you wish. Each car attaches to the tree.

> Materials: 1 piece hardboard, ⅛x4½x11-in.; copper wire or other hanging cord; yarn; self-adhesive plastic; spray sealer; primer; enamel paints.

1. Make a grid and draw the full-size patterns.

2. Transfer patterns to hardboard, either by tracing around a cardboard pattern or using carbon paper between the drawing and the hardboard.

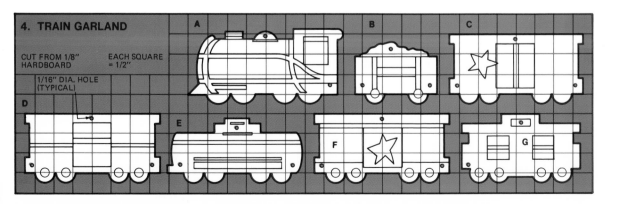

4. TRAIN GARLAND

CUT FROM 1/8"
HARDBOARD

EACH SQUARE
= 1/2"

1/16" DIA. HOLE
(TYPICAL)

3. Cut out cars using a sabre saw or jigsaw with a fine blade at low speed.

4. Using a ¹⁄₁₆-in.-dia. bit, bore holes in each car for connecting the cars together and for hanging them.

5. Spray on sealer, primer and enamel paint as directed in the general painting directions; sand, dust and wipe with a tack cloth between operations.

6. Cut out the self-adhesive plastic as shown or make your own designs. A paper punch makes small accent circles.

7. Join the cars with colored yarn.

8. Attach hanging wire or cord.

5 Horse ornament

These show horses are brightly painted and assembled with movable joints.

> Materials: 1 piece hardboard, ⅛x5x6 in.; 4 each brass paper fasteners with ¼-in. and ½-in. shanks; spray sealer; primer and red spray enamel; assorted acrylic paints; yarn; tiny screw eye or jewelry finding; hanging cord; tracing paper; graphite paper; white glue.

1. Make grid and draw full-size pattern on it.

2. Using graphite paper, transfer the pattern, outline only, to hardboard.

3. Mark and bore the holes for the paper fasteners.

4. Cut out the pieces using a sabre or jigsaw with a fine blade and slow feed rate.

5. Seal, prime and paint as discussed in general painting directions, sanding and dusting after each step but the final one.

6. Transfer the hoof, saddle and bridle designs onto the horse with graphite paper.

7. Paint the design backgrounds. Where two colors meet, let one color dry before painting the second color. Paint decorative dots on the bridle and saddle.

8. Assemble with paper fasteners as shown.

9. Glue on yarn mane and tail.

10. Bore hole for screw eye, making sure it is centered so the horse will remain balanced; attach screw eye and hang.

6 Punch-out ornaments

You can make these ornaments as colorful as you want.

> Materials: 1 piece plywood, ³⁄₁₆x4½x4½ in.; spray sealer; primer and assorted enamel paints; assorted enamels in jars; small paintbrush; hanging cord; carbon paper.

1. Make a grid and draw the full-size patterns on it.

2. Using carbon paper, transfer the outline and hole positions onto the hardboard.

3. Use a ⅛-in.-dia. bit to bore the holes.

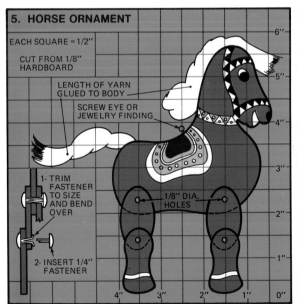

5. HORSE ORNAMENT
EACH SQUARE = 1/2"
CUT FROM 1/8" HARDBOARD
LENGTH OF YARN GLUED TO BODY
SCREW EYE OR JEWELRY FINDING
1- TRIM FASTENER TO SIZE AND BEND OVER
1/8" DIA. HOLES
2- INSERT 1/4" FASTENER

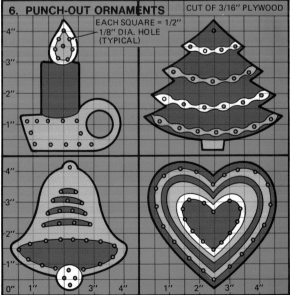

6. PUNCH-OUT ORNAMENTS
CUT OF 3/16" PLYWOOD
EACH SQUARE = 1/2"
1/8" DIA. HOLE (TYPICAL)

4. Cut out the pieces using a sabre or jigsaw with a fine blade and slow feed.

5. Spray sealer, primer and enamel on the shapes as mentioned in general painting directions, sanding, dusting and wiping with tack cloth between operations.

6. Decorate the ornaments with acrylic paints.

7. Hang with cord.

7 Heirloom rocker

One little rocking chair requires less than 70 in. of scrap cane binding (the wider cane material used around the edge of a chair).

Materials: 1 piece 7 in. cane binding (back); 1 piece 5¾ in. cane binding (seat); 2 pieces 5⅛ in. cane binding (arm); 2 pieces 8 in. cane binding (rocker); 2 pieces 4⅜ in. cane binding (side curl); 2 pieces 4¾ in. cane binding (back support); 2 pieces 1¾ in. cane binding (crosspiece); 1 piece 2¼ in. cane binding (oval); white glue; thread; scrap nylon stocking; indelible marker; modeling clay; cotton swabs; nail; bobby pin.

---

1. First soak the cane in warm water. Remove only the amount you can use at one time.

2. Cut the back piece (A). Color both sides with a marking pen. Since the cane is wet, the color will be subtle and will give an antique appearance. Shape the back; the bottom side should be 1⅜ in. wide. Overlap the cane ends near the bottom and glue. Then secure with thread.

7

3. Cut the seat (B). Color, and then bend in a square shape with each side measuring 1⅜-in. Overlap the ends ¼-in. Glue and bind with thread.

4. Cut, color and shape the arms (C), the rocker pieces (D) and the back supports (F). The arms and back supports both have curls. It is helpful to shape the curls around a nail, securing them for several minutes with bobby pins.

5. Upholster the back and seat with scrap nylon stocking. Begin work on the back by stretching a scrap of stocking over a mound of modeling clay that's been flattened in an area larger than the back. Secure the stocking on all sides of the work table. Apply glue with cotton swabs to the inside surface of the cane binding. Press the back into the stocking and clay and leave it until the glue dries. After an hour or so, remove the piece and trim off the excess stocking. Do the same with the rocker seat.

6. Glue and bind the arm, the rocker and the back support together, where they will attach to the back.

7. Glue and bind the arm and rocker at the bottom of the arm.

8. Glue and bind the bottom of the back support to the rocker.

9. Cut, color and shape the bottom side curls (E). Glue and bind them in place.

10. Glue the back to the side pieces, one at a time, by positioning a side piece on its side and balancing the back on it. (You can use the glue bottle and some cotton swabs taped to the bottle to prop the back until it dries.) **Note:** Inspect the assembly from all views to be sure the angles are correct.

11. Glue the seat to the assembly.

12. Cut, color and glue the bottom horizontal crosspieces (G).

13. Cut, color, glue and bind the oval (H). Then glue it in place.

8 Tinsel art Christmas tree

Tinsel art is an early-American craft. Our modern version uses crumpled tin foil to achieve a glittering effect.

Materials: 6 8½x11 in. picture frames; permanent felt-tip markers in black, light green, dark green, red, yellow, blue and orange; one tube of black acrylic paint; 1-in. wide paintbrush; large sheet of drawing paper; roll of aluminum foil.

---

1. Disassemble the picture frames; place the frame glass on drawing paper in a pyramid shape as shown in the illustration.

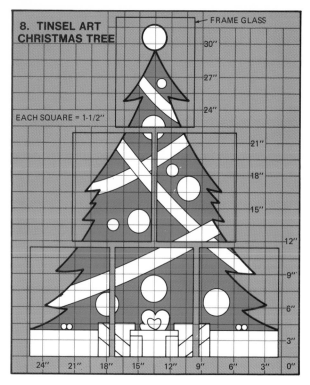

8. TINSEL ART CHRISTMAS TREE

FRAME GLASS

EACH SQUARE = 1-1/2"

30"
27"
24"
21"
18"
15"
12"
9"
6"
3"
0"

24" 21" 18" 15" 12" 9" 6" 3" 0"

2. Trace the outline of each piece of glass and put glass aside.

3. Lightly draw a grid over the outlines of the glass on the paper. Then draw the full-size Christmas tree pattern on the grid.

4. Place the glass on the pattern and outline the pattern on the glass with black marker. Fill in the outlines with colored markers.

5. Paint a black background around the tree on the glass with black acrylic paint. Let it dry.

6. Cut pieces of aluminum foil ¼-in. larger than the cardboard backings of the frames. Crumple, and then smooth out the foil pieces. Tape them to the backings, shiny side outward.

7. Reassemble the glass (painted side inward) and backings in the frame and hang.

10

9 Rainbow mobile

This colorful mobile can hang all year around.

> Materials: 1 piece pine, ¾x1½x16 in.; 1 piece pine ⅛x1⅛x12 in.; 1 piece pine ⅛x1⅛x11⅝ in.; 1 piece pine ⅛x1⅛x11¼ in.; 1 piece pine ⅛x1⅛x10⅞ in.; 1 piece pine ⅛x1⅛x10½ in.; 1 piece pine ⅛x1⅛x10⅛ in.; 1 piece pine ⅛x1⅛x9¾ in.; 1 piece pine ⅛x1⅛x9⅜ in.; 18 screw eyes; cord; graphite paper; sandpaper; pigmented shellac; acrylic paint in the following colors: light blue, black, white, red, orange, yellow, green, royal blue; medium small paint brush.

1. Cut wood pieces to size. Sand with 120-grit abrasive. Dust and wipe with tack cloth.

2. Prime-paint wood with pigmented shellac. Let dry, sand lightly with 180-grit paper, dust and wipe with a tack cloth.

3. Draw a grid to size and draw in rainbow pattern on tracing paper.

4. Clamp vertical parts together and transfer the rainbow pattern to the parts using graphite paper.

5. Outline the design using black acrylic paint and let dry overnight.

6. Paint sky background, rainbow and clouds on one side and edges, using the photo as a guide. Let dry.

7. Repeat steps 4 through 6 on other side.

8. Install screw eyes as shown; cut cord and assemble mobile.

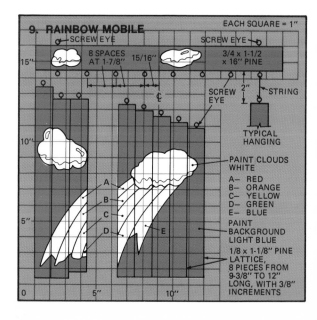

9. RAINBOW MOBILE

EACH SQUARE = 1"

SCREW EYE

SCREW EYE

15"

8 SPACES AT 1-7/8"   15/16"

3/4 x 1-1/2 x 16" PINE

SCREW EYE   2"   STRING

TYPICAL HANGING

PAINT CLOUDS WHITE

A— RED
B— ORANGE
C— YELLOW
D— GREEN
E— BLUE

PAINT BACKGROUND LIGHT BLUE

1/8 x 1-1/8" PINE LATTICE, 8 PIECES FROM 9-3/8" TO 12" LONG, WITH 3/8" INCREMENTS

10"

5"

A
B
C
D
E

0   5"   10"

10 Reindeer table decoration

The doe-eyed reindeer are so simple that you can make a herd at a time and use them as place-card props for Christmas dinner. Keep each in place with a pinch of modeling clay under the base.

> Materials: 1 piece hardboard, ⅛x9x1½ in. (antlers); 7½ in. of 1¼-in. dia dowel (large reindeer); 5⅜ in. of ⅞-in. dia. dowel (small reindeer); white glue; leather shoe string; ⅜- and ½-in. dia. plastic buttons; spray sealer; primer; brown and yellow enamels; red, blue, white acrylic paints; modeling clay.

1. Cut dowel parts; make the 90° base and muzzle cuts, and then make 30° cuts where the dowel pieces join.

2. Soften the edge of the muzzle with 120-grit abrasive. Round the area where the nose will be.

3. Glue the dowel parts together, hold parts with masking tape, and let dry.

4. Draw a full-size grid on paper or cardboard and draw the antler pattern over it. Trace onto hardboard.

5. Cut out using a sabre saw or jigsaw.

6. Secure the dowel assembly in a vise and bore holes for antlers and ears. Make a small V-cut where nose will be positioned.

7. Sand the wood smooth with 180-grit paper, dust, and wipe with a tack cloth.

8. Apply spray sealer, primer and two coats of Spanish Brown as directed in the general painting directions. Sand, dust and wipe with a tack cloth between operations.

9. Repeat steps 7 and 8 for the antlers using Marigold Yellow spray enamel.

10. Cut leather for the ears and secure in place with glue.

11. Paint eyes and lips.

12. Glue antlers and nose in place.

11 Santa's candy cane boot

This candy cane holder can hang on the wall or in front of the fireplace.

> Materials: 1 piece hardboard, ⅛x16x16 in.; one piece white fabric, 16x16 in.; contact cement; black felt-tip marker; red, yellow, orange, green, blue paint tubes, carbon paper, wall hanger.

1. Draw a full-size grid and draw the boot on the grid using plan here.

2. Transfer the boot outline onto hardboard. Either trace around a cardboard pattern or use carbon paper to trace a paper pattern.

3. Cut out the boot shape using sabre saw or jigsaw with a fine blade and a slow feed.

4. Trace the boot design onto white fabric. Then accent the lines with black marker.

5. Color the details with paint tubes, using the photo as a guide.

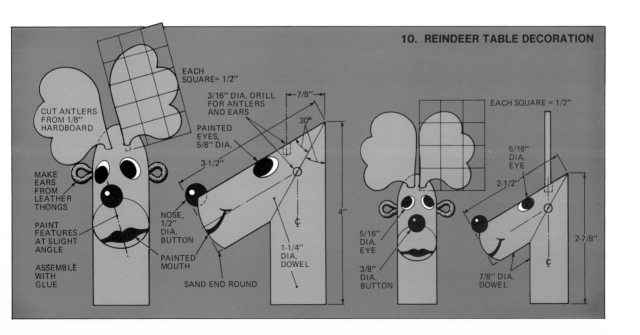

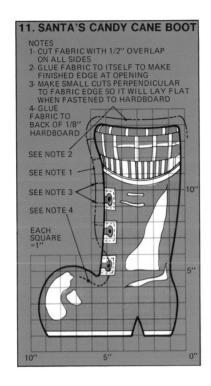

11. SANTA'S CANDY CANE BOOT

NOTES
1- CUT FABRIC WITH 1/2" OVERLAP ON ALL SIDES
2- GLUE FABRIC TO ITSELF TO MAKE FINISHED EDGE AT OPENING
3- MAKE SMALL CUTS PERPENDICULAR TO FABRIC EDGE SO IT WILL LAY FLAT WHEN FASTENED TO HARDBOARD
4- GLUE FABRIC TO BACK OF 1/8" HARDBOARD

SEE NOTE 2
SEE NOTE 1
SEE NOTE 3
SEE NOTE 4

EACH SQUARE =1"

10"
5"

10" 5" 0"

expose to air for 30 seconds, press parts together. Clamp immediately, dry overnight.

2. Trace body from pattern above, cut out, sand all edges.

3. Trace and cut out wings. Locate entry point for brads. Nip off head of a brad one size smaller than the ⅞-in. brads used and use it to bore pilot holes for the attaching brads in the wings and body. Sand parts smooth, dust, wipe with tack cloth.

4. Bore candle hole.

5. Sand parts smooth, dust and wipe with tack cloth.

6. Seal, prime and spray paint according to general painting directions.

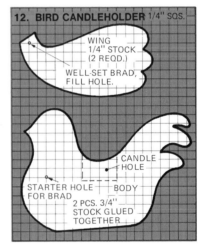

12. BIRD CANDLEHOLDER 1/4" SQS.

WING 1/4" STOCK (2 REQD.)
WELL-SET BRAD, FILL HOLE.
CANDLE HOLE
STARTER HOLE FOR BRAD
BODY
2 PCS. 3/4" STOCK GLUED TOGETHER

6. Cut out the boot leaving a ½-in. border.

7. Make a perpendicular cut into the border every inch to form tabs around the boot fabric. **Note:** Do not cut tabs on the top edge of the fabric. Cut the tabs on the sides near the top of the boot somewhat shallower than the lower tabs to allow some slack when attaching the fabric to the hardboard.

8. Hem the top edge of the boot fabric with contact cement. Apply contact cement to the underside of the tabs and bend them around to fasten at the back of the hardboard. Allow slack when attaching the side tabs near the top. Let dry.

9. Place a hanger on the back. Then fill the boot with candy canes.

12 Bird candleholders

Materials for each bird: ¼x2x3¾-in. piece of lattice for each wing; 2 pieces ¾x4x5-in. stock glued together for body; ⅞-in. brads, white glue, plastic wood filler, sealer, primer, antique white spray enamel.

1. Cut ¾-in. stock to length; glue up pieces for body. Apply glue sparingly to mating surfaces;

12

7. When paint is dry, affix wings to body with glue and brads. Support wings if necessary until glue dries (overnight).

8. Fill brad holes with plastic wood filler, let dry and sand smooth. Touch up with paint.

13 Tree of life candleholder

> Materials: heavy duty funnel; 1⅜-in. dia. dowel; ⅜-in. dia. dowel; 3/16-in. balsawood; light-gauge wire; drapery finial top; 4, ⅝-in. No. 4 rh wood screws; 12, ¼-in. No. 2 fh wood screws; 12 sliding-door flush pulls; white glue; sealant; primer; white, red and green spray enamel.

1. Cut funnel as required. Bore four holes through funnel equally spaced near the top opening. Cut 1⅜-in.-dia. dowel to size and position in funnel. Mark entry position for four screws to secure funnel to dowel. Bore holes in funnel and dowel and attach screws.

2. Mark and bore holes in large dowel for smaller dowel branches. Cut dowel branches and bore small holes in them at random to later attach wired leaves and apples. Leave room at ends for door pulls to hold candles.

3. Bore holes for screws to attach door pull candleholders; slide branches in place and glue. Attach door pulls.

4. Bore hole and attach finial.

5. Seal, prime and paint tree white as explained in general painting directions.

6. Cut apples and leaves out of balsawood. Make a small hole for attachment wire with an awl and glue wire. Seal, prime and spray paint. Glue leaves and apples in place.

14 Tree candleholder centerpiece

> Materials: ⅜-in.-dia. dowel (2 pieces 4¾-in. and 4 pieces 3 in); 1 block of wood 4¾ in. sq. x 10 in.; 4 blocks 4 in. sq. x 10 in.; 2 blocks 3½ in. x 6 in.; sealer; primer; green spray-enamel paint.

1. Glue up wood to create blocks for turning.

2. Turn blocks in lathe as indicated to make two small trees (S), four medium trees (M) and one large tree (L).

3. Bore candleholding hole while tree is in lathe. Or clamp tree to drill-press table to bore hole at center.

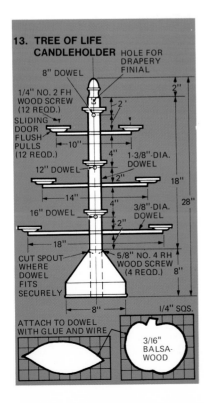

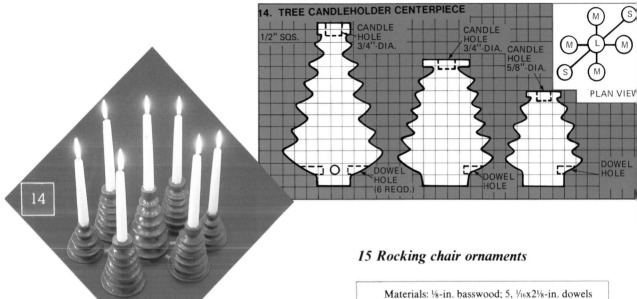

14. TREE CANDLEHOLDER CENTERPIECE

1/2" SQS.

CANDLE HOLE 3/4"-DIA.

CANDLE HOLE 3/4"-DIA.

CANDLE HOLE 5/8"-DIA.

DOWEL HOLE (6 REQD.)

DOWEL HOLE

DOWEL HOLE

PLAN VIEW

14

4. Bore holes for dowels on tree bases as marked. Use scrap wood beneath each tree plus hand screw clamps to assure tree being level (90° to drill bit).

5. Seal, sand and then finish by applying several coats of green spray enamel. Sand lightly between coats and wipe with tack cloth before applying next coat.

15 Rocking chair ornaments

Materials: 1/8-in. basswood; 5, 1/16x2 1/8-in. dowels for back; 2, 1/16x2 1/4-in. dowels for back; 4, 1/16x5/8-in. dowels for arms; 4, 3/8x1 1/8-in. dowels for legs; 2, 1/16x7/8-in. dowels for leg crosspieces; white glue; sealant; primer; spray enamel and bottled enamel paints.

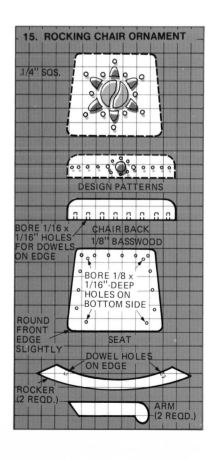

15. ROCKING CHAIR ORNAMENT

1/4" SQS.

DESIGN PATTERNS

BORE 1/16 x 1/16" HOLES FOR DOWELS ON EDGE

CHAIR BACK 1/8" BASSWOOD

BORE 1/8 x 1/16"-DEEP HOLES ON BOTTOM SIDE

ROUND FRONT EDGE SLIGHTLY

SEAT

DOWEL HOLES ON EDGE

ROCKER (2 REQD.)

ARM (2 REQD.)

15

1. Cut all dowels and basswood pieces. Sand edges smooth.

2. Use an awl or nail to bore holes for attaching dowels on chair back, arms, seat (top and under sides) and rockers.

3. Glue the two long dowels at the ends of the chair back with the five shorter dowels in between. Let the glue set several minutes and glue these dowels to the seat.

4. Glue the arm dowels into the arm and glue this assembly to the back and seat.

5. Glue the rocker assembly together. Let it set somewhat, then glue the cross dowels in place.

6. Glue the rocker and seat assemblies together.

7. After glue dries, seal, prime and paint following general painting directions.

16 Candy cane candleholder

> Materials: 1⅛x7-in.-dia. pine base; 1⅜-in.-dia. dowels; ¾-in.-dia. dowels; 7 small baby food jar lids; Super Glue; satin polyurethane varnish; primer; green and white spray enamel paints; ½-in.-wide red vinyl tape.

1. Cut pine base. Mark off dowel placement and bore holes ¼-in. deep. Sand base smooth.

2. Cut dowels to size. Varnish and paint dowels white or leave natural as indicated on plan. Wind red vinyl tape around white dowels for candy stripe effect.

3. Glue dowels into base.

4. Spray paint jar lids green, glue lids in place, add candle cups and candles.

17 Wall sconce

> Materials: ⁷⁄₁₆-in. oak or other hardwood; prismatic film; ⅞-in. brass candle cup and 2-in.-dia. brass candle plate; ½-in. No. 6 rh screw and washer; 2, 1-in. No. 6 fh screws; dark wood stain; polyurethane clear finish; white glue.

1. Cut wood pieces, stain and apply finish.

2. Mark prismatic film patterns on backing, checking that star patterns coincide on longer film cutouts. Use utility knife to cut.

16. CANDY CANE CANDLEHOLDER

1-1/4 x 7"-DIA. PINE DISC

BABY FOOD JAR CAP (7 REQD.)

TOP VIEW

1" SQS.

BORE 1/4"-DEEP HOLES FOR DOWELS AND GLUE

WRAP 3/4"-WIDE RED VINYL TAPE AROUND DOWEL FOR CANDY STRIPE

15-3/4"

12-1/2"

9-1/2"

6-3/4"

A
1-3/8"
DOWEL

B
3/4"
DOWEL
(2 REQD.)

C
3/4"
DOWEL
(2 REQD.)

D
1-3/8"
DOWEL
(4 REQD.)

16

3. Trace window outlines lightly on wood for proper placement. Peel off backing and press film; it will adhere instantly.

4. Attach the base to the back with glue and screws. Secure candle cup and plate. Bore hole to hang sconce.

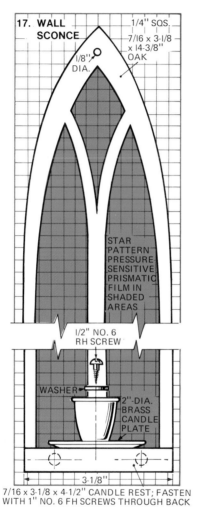

17. **WALL SCONCE**
1/4" SQS.
7/16 x 3-1/8 x 14-3/8" OAK
1/8" DIA.
STAR PATTERN PRESSURE SENSITIVE PRISMATIC FILM IN SHADED AREAS
1/2" NO. 6 RH SCREW
WASHER
2"-DIA. BRASS CANDLE PLATE
3-1/8"
7/16 x 3-1/8 x 4-1/2" CANDLE REST; FASTEN WITH 1" NO. 6 FH SCREWS THROUGH BACK

4. Hand-paint decorations on strainer band and vinyl tape.

5. Attach Christmas tree hook. Glue on mailing label and cut to flag shape.

17

18 Balloon ornaments

> Materials: gutter strainer; 1x1⅜-in. dia. dowel; 1-in.-wide colored vinyl tape; white glue, acrylic paints in several colors; Christmas tree hook; adhesive mailing label to make top flag.

1. Cut dowel to length.
2. Shape gutter strainer around dowel.
3. Secure with white glue and colored tape.

18

19. Plastic tree ornaments are rings of plastic tubing with decorations embedded in resin poured inside.

20 Santa Claus window hanging

Materials: 1/8x9-in.-dia. acrylic disc. (Have this cut by your supplier.) You'll also need a flexible-shaft tool with these attachments: tungsten carbide cutter to cut outlines; small round engraving cutter for detail work; twist drill to bore hanging hole; plus an indelible-ink felt-tip pen to transfer drawing.

19 Plastic tree ornaments

Materials: 3-in.-dia. clear or colored acrylic tubing cut into 1/2-in. rings; clear casting resin and catalyst; embedments such as dried flowers, pine cones and evergreen, hangers. You'll also need a dowel or other stirring stick, 2-lb. coffee can or other container that can be discarded (or use a plastic bowl—dried resin will chip off it); medium and fine-grit sandpaper; aluminum foil; felt polishing pad and polishing wheel; polishing compound for plastics; cement used on plastics. Work in a well-ventilated area.

1. Cut tubing rings.

2. Spread aluminum foil on flat surface, and place clean, dry tubing rings on it.

3. Be sure coffee tin or other mixing container is clean and dry. Carefully measure out resin—use about 1/2 lb. for every two tubing molds. Carefully measure out the amount of catalyst noted in the manufacturer's directions and stir.

4. Fill the mold halfway with resin. Hold the mold with one hand while you pour. Let it cure. (Temperature may reach 150° during this time so be careful where you place it.)

5. After first layer has cured (it will take two hours to become sticky, but let it cure until completely hard), position embedments. Make pine cone flower by positioning petals individually in circle shape, overlapping in several layers.

6. Again mix resin and catalyst; fill molds to top—almost overflowing (steps 3 and 4). This layer will fill places where the first layer has shrunk away from the tubing.

7. After resin has cured, lift away from aluminum foil, sand and polish rough edges.

8. Bore a small hole at top for hanger and secure it with cement used on plastics.

20. SANTA WINDOW HANGING
(RIGHT SIDE IS MIRROR IMAGE)
1/4" SQS.

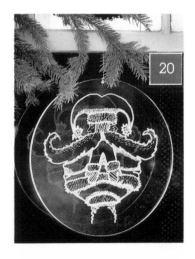

20

1. Enlarge design. Place it under the acrylic disc and draw design on disc with felt-tip pen.

2. With carbide cutter in hobbyist's tool, go over all lines as if retracing them.

3. Use same cutter and round engraving cutter to give texture where areas are darkened on plan.

4. Use twist drill accessory to bore hole for hanging.

5. Polish away pen markings with toothpaste on a soft cloth.

21 Wreath window hanging

> Materials: clear casting resin and catalyst; embedments such as pine boughs, cone, dried flowers; hanger. You'll also need a frozen-pie tin; dowel stirring stick; coffee tin or bowl that can be discarded; flexible-shaft tool with tungsten carbide cutter. Work in a well-ventilated area.

21

1. Carefully pour about 2 lbs. resin into bowl and add catalyst according to directions on package; mix.

2. Pour half the mixture into the clean, dry pie tin.

3. Position the embedments in the resin.

4. Slowly, so as not to disturb the embedments, pour rest of resin in the tin. Use mixing stick to submerge the embedments if needed.

5. Allow the resin to cure (it may heat up to 150°, so use care in placing it). When it is hard and completely cured—it will be cool—remove it from the tin.

6. Sand off rough edges.

7. If you add a greeting, first mark it on the disc with an indelible felt-tip pen.

8. With a tool and tungsten cutter retrace the pen lines.

9. Remove excess pen marks with toothpaste and a soft cloth.

10. With twist-drill accessory in flexible-shaft tool, bore a small hole for the hanger on disc top. Cement hanger in place.

22 Wood-ring candlesticks

Holders shown are made of wood sections available at craft shops.

Crescent holder

> Materials: 1″ i.d. wood ring, 16 crescents less than half circle with 2 to 2½″ o.d., metal candle spike, spray sealer, acrylic paint, white glue.

Seal and paint wood. Assemble holder upside down in small bowl, starting with ring. Glue ends of four crescents to ring. Make four layers of four crescents each. When dry, remove from bowl; glue spike to ring.

Loop-the-loop holder

> Materials: two 2¼″ i.d. rings, 1½″ i.d. ring, three 1″ i.d. rings, spray sealer, acrylic paint and white glue.

Seal and paint rings. Glue two small ones together and two large ones together. Lay the me-

dium ring on a table and glue larger ones upright on it. Glue a small ring upright inside large ones and place double small rings horizontally on large ones.

Wood-ring spandrel holder

> Materials: 1¾″ i.d. ring, three 1¼″ i.d. rings, 3 medium-size triangular spandrels, spray sealer, acrylic paint, white glue.

Seal and paint wood. Glue spandrels in triangular shape, corners touching. Glue large rings on top, followed by remaining rings.

Rattan holder

> Materials: 2¼″ i.d. wood ring, two 1¼″ i.d. rings, 3 crescents less than a half circle from 2¾ to 3¾″ o.d., spray varnish, white glue.

Varnish wood. Glue ends of three crescents to large ring to form a triangle. Glue two small rings together; then glue them to crescent tops.

23 Star candleholders

> Materials for one star: 5 pieces ¾ x 7¼ x 8″ clear pine, carpenter's glue, 180-grit abrasive paper, oil stain, varnish, scented candle in cup.

Apply glue to mating surfaces of five pieces of pine and clamp. Immediately, wipe off all glue squeeze-out with damp cloth. Let clamped star dry overnight. Using pattern above as guide, draw free-form star on block's top surface. Cut out star with bandsaw. On star top, mark somewhat larger dimensions than candle cup and bore its hole. Using 2¼″ multispur bit or holesaw, bore holes through each valley junction of star. *Caution:* Be sure star is aligned perfectly and clamped securely to drillpress table.

To finish, sand lightly with 180-grit paper, dust and apply choice of stain following maker's instructions. Let stain dry overnight, then apply thinned coat of semigloss varnish diluted 50 percent with turpentine. Let dry 24 hours, then apply varnish from the can. As the candle burns, light will shine through the holes.

24. STAINED GLASS WINDOW HANGING

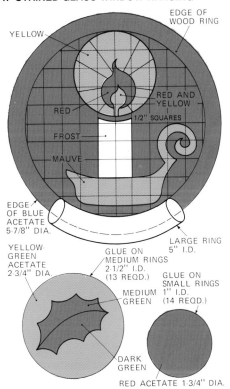

23. STAR CANDLEHOLDER

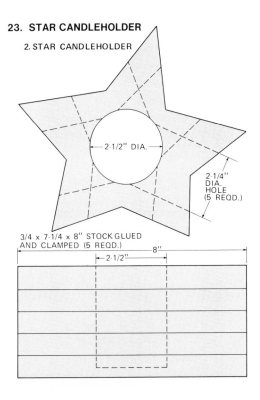

24 Stained-glass window hanging

> Materials: 14 1″ i.d. wood rings, 13 2½″ i.d. rings, 5″ i.d. ring, bottle liquid lead, model glue; spray sealer, glossy white spray paint, one sheet each of these acetates: yellow-green, medium and dark green, red, frost, yellow, mauve, blue.

Angel

Frost border by rubbing with medium-grit sand-paper after taping off clear area. Etch outline with a carbide-tipped scriber. Finish as above.

Deer-tree decoration

This requires a hand-grinder-type power tool. Etch tree with scriber or power tool with cutter accessory—deeply for foregrounds; lightly for backgrounds. Etch deer with round steel burs in power tool. Begin with large burs and work to small burs. Finish as above.

Santa-tree decoration

Etch the entire design with large and small burs in a power tool and finish.

Draw design full scale according to plan. Seal and paint wood rings. Draw and cut out the blue, yellow-green and red disc shapes and other colored acetate shapes to be inlaid. From large and medium discs, cut out areas where inlays will be placed. Glue disc shapes of acetate to underside of the appropriate rings.

Center the large ring on an 18½-in. square piece of frosted acetate backing for reinforcement. Space small rings around the large one, glue to the backing and then glue rings together at their contact points. Position medium rings and glue them to backing and small rings. Arrange remaining colored acetate shapes on discs and tack-glue. Squeeze liquid lead in a line around color borders. Attach cord and hang.

25 and 26 Acrylic decorations

Materials: ⅛" acrylic plastic, indelible ink marker, red and white polishing rouge.

Beginning and finishing procedures are similar for all decorations. Cut the plastic with jigsaw or sabre saw to the shapes shown. Draw design on acrylic. Etch design in plastic as described below. For the finish, polish plastic to remove ink with either red and white rouge or toothpaste on a soft cloth. Wash with mild liquid soap.

27 Macramé wall-hanging Christmas tree

Materials: 60-yd., 5-ply, 28-lb. ball of green jute twine, 2″ metal ring, 20 red 20-mm large-holed wood beads, two 28-mm large-holed natural wood beads, ⅜″ dia. x 16″ wood dowel, 2 yds. red cord or yarn, 18 x 24″ Styrofoam knotting board, T-pins, white glue.

Cut the cords to size and tie them to wood dowel as shown. Begin tying by making a square knot with the first four cords. Repeat with the next four cords. Complete first row of nine knots.

In second row skip the first two cords at left and join cords three and four with cords five and six to tie a square knot as shown above. Continue along this row (eight knots), leaving two free cords at each end.

Continue this alternating knot pattern in row three by taking cords one and two (not used in previous row) and knotting them again with cords three and four. Complete row (nine knots).

In row four begin to decrease the knots by tying one less square knot every *fourth* row. Slip red beads on the spare two cords on both ends. In the fourth row slip beads between knots two and three, four and five, six and seven. To complete design, continue to decrease or drop two cords on both ends each fourth row. Add red bead in triangular design to accent tree shape.

At the top of the tree, secure the eight cords around a metal ring with red cord and trim. Turn the tree over and pull the beaded side cords through adjacent knots, glue and trim. Attach eight 12-in. cords in the center of the wood dowel, secure them with red cord and trim, glue large beads on the dowel ends.

28 Glittering tree decorations

Materials: ⅛″ balsa wood, acrylic spray paint, metalized film with adhesive backing (sometimes called defraction trim; available at hobby and automotive accessory shops).

Using a utility knife, cut trees, circles or other shapes out of balsa wood and spray-paint. When dry, apply shiny trim cut in small circles, squares or narrow strips. Pass a needle through the balsa to thread it for hanging.

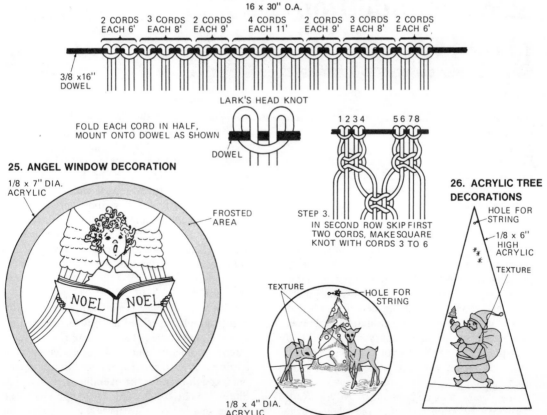

27. CHRISTMAS TREE WALL HANGING

16 x 30″ O.A.

2 CORDS EACH 6′ 3 CORDS EACH 8′ 2 CORDS EACH 9′ 4 CORDS EACH 11′ 2 CORDS EACH 9′ 3 CORDS EACH 8′ 2 CORDS EACH 6′

3/8 x16″ DOWEL

LARK'S HEAD KNOT

FOLD EACH CORD IN HALF, MOUNT ONTO DOWEL AS SHOWN

DOWEL

1 2 3 4   5 6 7 8

STEP 3. IN SECOND ROW SKIP FIRST TWO CORDS, MAKE SQUARE KNOT WITH CORDS 3 TO 6

25. ANGEL WINDOW DECORATION

1/8 x 7″ DIA. ACRYLIC

FROSTED AREA

NOEL NOEL

1/8 x 4″ DIA. ACRYLIC

TEXTURE

HOLE FOR STRING

26. ACRYLIC TREE DECORATIONS

HOLE FOR STRING

1/8 x 6″ HIGH ACRYLIC

TEXTURE

Room addition planning

■ **HOW MANY TIMES** have you wished you could alter the layout of your house? Whether it's relocating a door or closet, widening a hall or raising a roof, most houses have an area that should and could have been planned better. If you're thinking about an addition, now's the time to consider all your options and work all the bugs out of the plan.

The first step is to find out any limits you must work within. Your assessors' office may have a tax map for your area that shows the size of your property and location of your house. Get a few copies so you know what you're working with. Next, ask your local building department about limitations on yard spaces around your house. Most codes specify how close you can build to your property line. When you get these figures, lay them out on your tax map using the map scale.

Now you have some boundaries. As you think about your addition—how big and where it will be—pencil it in on the map adjoining the house. Even though you may be planning your dream room, remember that you may be giving up something like a shade tree or natural runoff for ground water. Make sure you locate the septic tank and underground piping such as a gas line. There are horror stories about porches with special cuts, fittings and hinges to get at the septic tank that was forgotten when the porch was built. Balance your wildest dreams with a practical solution and pick the best site available.

Make the first plan

Start working on a larger scale. Get a pad of ¼-inch graph paper and lay out the dimensions of your house, one square for one foot. Include interior room sizes and mark door openings. Put a thin piece of tracing paper over this and sketch out a rough plan for the overall size of your addition. Do one sketch of the biggest and best, one of the smallest, and as many variations as you can think of in between. Even if you decide that you don't like the overall idea in a drawing, keep it. You may find it contains a good idea that you'll wind up incorporating in the final plan.

The easy way to move furniture

Take some colored construction paper and measure out, to scale, the approximate sizes of furniture you expect to use in a room. Pick out a few sketches you like best and try different furniture arrangements on them. This is likely to cut down on the number of designs because you'll find some layouts are a natural for the furniture you have in mind—and some just won't work at all. Now go back to the graph paper and put in more details. Locate windows, closets and doors exactly, and the thickness of all interior walls (figure 4 to 5 inches to scale). If your sketch starts to look messy, retrace it on a clean sheet of paper.

You'll have to compromise

Here come the first big decisions. The easiest way to compromise is to multiply the total floor area of your addition by a per-square-foot cost estimate. This figure can be obtained by talking to new homeowners and builders in your area. If you contemplate using expensive materials like plaster, tile, parquet floors and hardwood cabinets, you'd better add an additional amount to the figure. This system makes it somewhat easier to eliminate your more elaborate designs. Your addition should be just what you want, but it should also be practical and it has to be affordable or you'll have no addition at all.

Make the second plan

Here are some new rules. They'll save construction time and material costs. If you're figuring the width of a room at 17 feet, try 16. This way, two sheets of 4×8 plywood and 16-foot joists will fit. You'll be saving a bundle on materials by eliminating waste. Get a copy of local building codes or contact your building inspector. You may find that by making your room 6 inches narrower you can use 2×8 joists instead of 2×10s. Before you put all this into a final plan, find out about materials. See what's available at local lumberyards. Get some catalogs (with prices) and look at flooring, tile, windows and doors. You may find a good-looking siding that comes in 4-foot widths. It eliminates the need for plywood sheathing (in most areas) and will cut costs considerably. This may buy you back that extra few feet of space you want in the room.

A time for final decisions

Hopefully you've picked your location and you should have a sketch that's very close to the final plan. Considering materials, costs, availability and your needs, make the last adjustments and draw the final sketch neatly. Before proceeding with a contractor or starting the job if you're doing it yourself, make an appointment with the building inspector. Their job is to be sure you live in a safe, secure house, so take their advice.

Don't rush it

Take your time with planning. Give yourself an opportunity to make mistakes now, on paper. Moving a wall later on is expensive. Since you're going to live in the addition, you're really better equipped than anyone else to plan its layout. Even if you expect to see an architect for a design, you'll have something specific to show that reflects your needs.

How will it look? If may be difficult to visualize the elevation from a floor plan. Drawing a simple elevation of each exposed side will help. Work from dimensions on your plan to get the length of each wall. It's important that the addition looks like part of the house; not like a box stuck against it. So make the heights of all doors, windowsills and fascias the same as they are in the house. Sticking with the same siding and paint color helps, and definitely use the same color shingles.

For your drawings, get dimensions from your existing house and transfer them, to scale, to your elevations. Orient the drawings by marking each one north, south, east or west elevation. If you are really ambitious, use the plan dimensions to build a scale model.

Take your time. Make a good plan now, and you won't want to change anything after it's built.

Add on to your home and save

■ THAT BEAUTIFUL vacation home in the mountains may soon be outgrown by the flow of guests and the increasing size of your family. You may soon find you need more space for sleeping and privacy, as well as a place for your cars. You may also want to add central heating to open up possibilities for winter weekend visits to that vacation home.

Homeowners in this situation face two choices: They can (1) sell the original house and build something more spacious elsewhere, or (2) find a way to add on to the existing house.

After careful analysis of finances and costs, you may find that a wing would provide what

L-WING ADDITION (above) extends at a right angle from the porch end of original cottage. What it did for the living space is shown in diagram (below). The original house is above. New wing is from far end of porch.

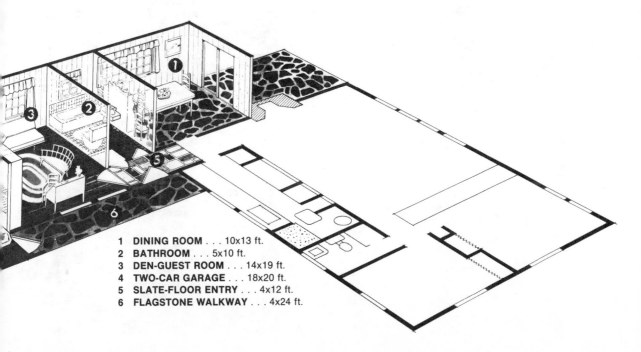

1 **DINING ROOM** . . . 10x13 ft.
2 **BATHROOM** . . . 5x10 ft.
3 **DEN-GUEST ROOM** . . . 14x19 ft.
4 **TWO-CAR GARAGE** . . . 18x20 ft.
5 **SLATE-FLOOR ENTRY** . . . 4x12 ft.
6 **FLAGSTONE WALKWAY** . . . 4x24 ft.

FLOOR JOISTS ARE sunk into foundation wall and rest on a sill along the ledge formed by top course of 4-in. block. This, plus use of 7-ft. 9½-in. sidewalls, permits using 4x8-ft. panel siding.

WALL SECTIONS are assembled and joined on the subfloor decking, then tipped up into final position.

FIBERBOARD SHEATHING panels are snubbed right against the rafters and fastened with 2-in. nails.

GABLE END RAFTERS are cut and assembled on the ground, then lifted into place and braced. Care must be taken to insure peak is exactly same height from bottom cord as trusses. Studs can be cut to fit.

you need for approximately half the cost of a new home with the same facilities—provided you can do most of the work yourself.

You do need help with some things—handling heavy trusses, raising ceiling panels, closing in the roof before the rains come, and so on. You can contract the foundation hole. Your local electrical contractor can relocate the primary electrical service box, and the manufacturer or dealer will most likely install the furnace. Friendly relatives and friends can be pressed into service in this kind of a vacation home project, often with little more reward than the promise of an invitation to come visit when it is finished.

The extension wing shown here can be added to almost any house of one or two floors if the land to put it on is available and meets code requirements. The important factor is to take your time in planning the addition so that it looks like part of the original structure and not a "tack-on." The roof design and pitch must be carefully considered to fit in. If they follow the original, you're safe. On most homes, and especially those with shallow pitch or flat roofs, an "L" wing may even improve the building's appearance by spreading it out and blending with the landscape.

The framing in the wing of the house shown is similar in design to the original house. A stepped foundation wall is used in which the last course of block is 4 in. wide. Joists rest on a sill behind the top row. This stunt lowers the house into the foundation wall, permitting the use of standard 4×8-ft. panels for sheathing and siding.

A single, 44-ft.-long, doubled-up 2×12 header supports the roof trusses across the long spans of garage doors and between the posts at the front.

Roof and sidewalls were tied into the existing house after erection—but before interior surfaces were covered. The critical task of making a waterproof joint where the roofs meet is all important if you want a dry home.

The work on the addition here took one and a half years. Two months of weekends were used just replacing windows in the original house to match those in the new wing. The original house also had to be resurfaced with the new fiberglass siding to match the new wing. When it was done, the owners gained an additional 972 sq. ft. of enclosed space including:

• **A cedar-paneled dining room** occupying half of a former patio in the original ranch-type house. The flagstone deck from the patio was left as a handsome floor. It was filled with sealer and polished with Butcher's wax. A 6-ft.-wide sliding

glass door faces the remaining half of the patio.
• **A full bath** lined with gray fiberglass barn siding, and white fixtures as a contrast. The tub stall is walled in gray epoxy panels to shed water from the shower head.
• **A den-guest room** paneled in natural cedar. The room includes built-in shelves and cabinets, which flank a prefab fireplace. The floor is waxed, random oak planking. A sofa bed can turn the entire room into an extra bedroom to accommodate a weekend guest couple in roomy comfort. It can also be used as an office or den when you're alone. With very little additional work or expense, you can turn it into a luxurious master bedroom.
• **A two-car garage** that could be stretched to 20×20 ft. by simply extending the rear wall out under the 2-ft. roof overhang. This might be a good idea if you're a "big car" fan, or want to install a workbench and work area.
• **A redwood-paneled entry,** with random slate-flag floor. This is good-looking and practical for a vacation home where country mud and slush can easily be cleaned away. Backing into the bath area from this hall is a 26×34-in. coat closet with shelves and bins for boots, storm lamps and other useful items that are likely to be needed in a vacation home.

• **A 4-ft.-wide covered walk** outside, paved in random flagstone. This parallels the entry hall between the house entrance and a door leading into the garage. Since this is covered, it offers the convenience of getting from the house to the car without getting soaked.
• **An oil-fired, hot-air heating system** that provides balanced heat throughout the new wing as well as the original part of the building. Since both original house and wing sit on shallow bedrock over a tight crawlspace, the problem of a proper furnace seemed like a rough one at first. Actually, the solution was easy. Most manufacturers produce "horizontal" furnaces designed to fit beneath floor joists where clearance is as little as 2 ft. Plenum and ductwork come off one end.

The satisfaction of watching a house grow under your own hands can never be appreciated by anyone who hasn't built one, and it's not as hard as you may think. You'll learn many techniques that help speed up the work as you go along and by asking local professionals for hints and advice.

With the addition completed, you can spend even more time at your vacation home and entertain more guests. It takes careful planning and a lot of weekends, but the results are worth it.

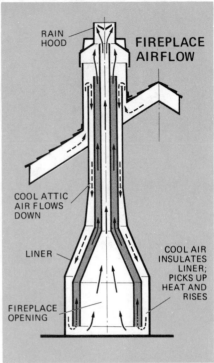

RAIN HOOD

FIREPLACE AIRFLOW

COOL ATTIC AIR FLOWS DOWN

LINER

COOL AIR INSULATES LINER; PICKS UP HEAT AND RISES

FIREPLACE OPENING

PACKAGED FIREPLACE (above) can be set on a wood floor, backed against a flammable wall with no fire hazard. Triple-pipe flue (right) is cooled by air. Cutaway of fireplace assembly (above, right) shows how the circulation of cool air between the two layers of steel provides insulation for outer surface.

HORIZONTAL FURNACE, designed to fit the 24-inch clearance in tight crawlspace, puts out enough B.T.U. to heat an eight-room house.

Expand over an attached garage

■ WHEN YOU EXPAND over an existing structure, you save a lot of trouble and expense. The basic foundation is already there, and, in some cases, so is the floor. You simply build upward on top, avoiding many of the headaches of starting from scratch.

Here is a two-stage improvement project that starts with the attached garage:

• The first improvement adds a family room, complete with wood-burning fireplace, alongside the garage.

• The second builds over the garage to gain a master bedroom away from the existing four bedrooms.

The new wing, which permits construction of a private bath and sitting room as well as bedroom, also has sliding doors for access to a deck over the new family room.

A cathedral ceiling was created of rough-hewn cedar. The rafters were left exposed and stained. The entire room is paneled to eliminate future painting.

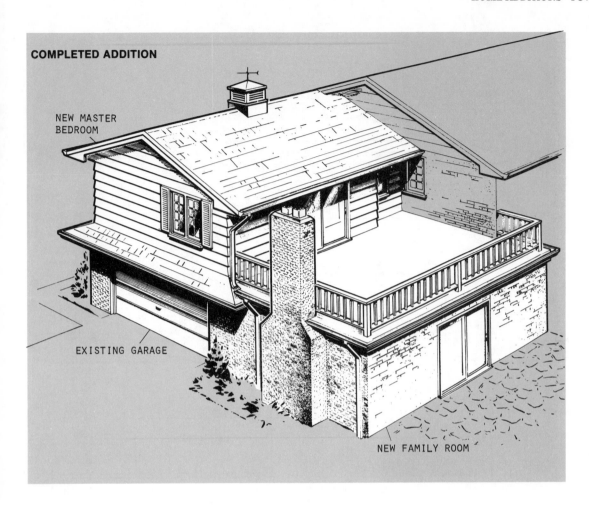

COMPLETED ADDITION

NEW MASTER BEDROOM

EXISTING GARAGE

NEW FAMILY ROOM

Outside, the roof pitch follows the existing structure. The result is that the addition does not look tacked on but gives the appearance of having always been there. To keep cost down, aluminum siding was used, rather than the brick veneer on the rest of the house.

Expanding up, when possible, rather than attaching a new structure is a practical approach to home improvement for several reasons. It is more economical because the footings under the garage are already there. Excavation and concrete work are not required and, if you desire, that money can be put toward interior luxuries or extras. Expanding up also leaves more yard area for outdoor activities.

Whether you decide to add both rooms in one project, only one, or one now and the second as time and money permit, the building concept shown here is a sound one. Once either or both additions are closed to the weather, interior work can proceed as you—not the elements—dictate.

COLONIAL HOME (below) was adequate when the family first moved in. When more room was needed, a bedroom was added over the garage and a playroom alongside.

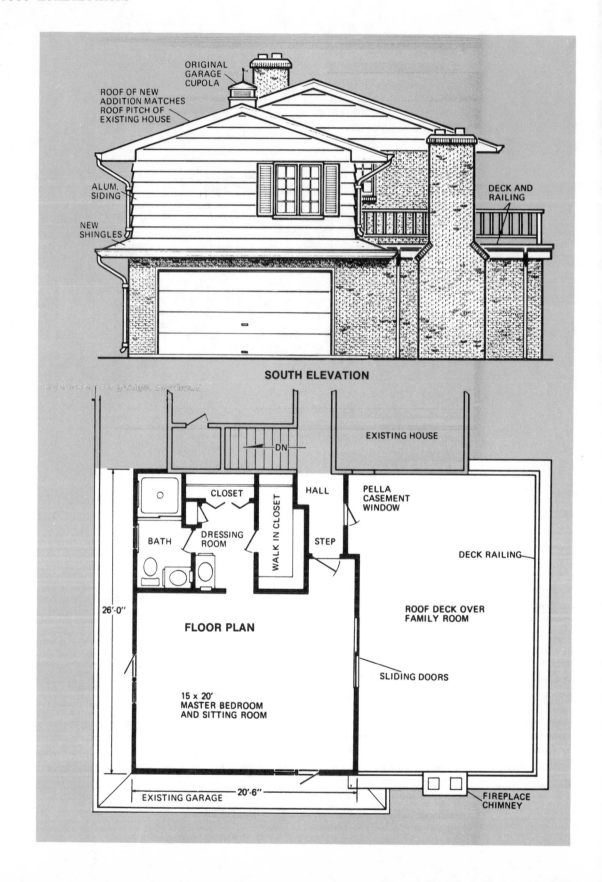

ORIGINAL GARAGE CUPOLA

ROOF OF NEW ADDITION MATCHES ROOF PITCH OF EXISTING HOUSE

ALUM. SIDING

NEW SHINGLES

DECK AND RAILING

SOUTH ELEVATION

DN

EXISTING HOUSE

CLOSET

HALL

PELLA CASEMENT WINDOW

BATH

DRESSING ROOM

WALK IN CLOSET

STEP

DECK RAILING

26'-0"

FLOOR PLAN

ROOF DECK OVER FAMILY ROOM

SLIDING DOORS

15 x 20' MASTER BEDROOM AND SITTING ROOM

EXISTING GARAGE

20'-6"

FIREPLACE CHIMNEY

Home improvement projects

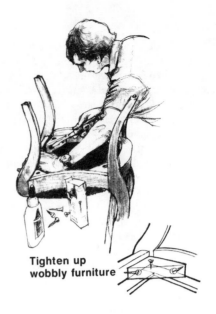

Tighten up wobbly furniture

Tighten up wobbly furniture

You and your guests will want to sit comfortably—not in chairs that have the shakes. Chairs built with corner-block construction, like the one shown, may require no more than tightening the screws in the blocks. For other chairs, you can make corner blocks to hold those loose joints together—install them with white glue and screws. Note angled holes to let screws enter frame squarely. L-shaped or notched blocks can also be used.

Fix sticking doors

Planing may be the only way to ease a binding door; clamping it to a wooden box is a good way to hold it—don't forget to cut hinge mortises back to original depth afterward. But you can try other remedies before you take the door down. If the bind is at the threshold, put coarse sandpaper there and swing the door over it. Loose hinges can make a door stick, so tighten hinge screws. If you find a free-turning screw in an enlarged hole, you can anchor it in a rolled-up scrap of metal toothpaste tube.

Fix sticking doors

Put up a wainscot

Wainscoting is an attractive improvement—and a convenient coverup if the lower part of a wall is in bad shape. Kit type is easy to install with adhesive, nails, and clips between tongue-and-groove panels. The chair-rail molding at the top protects the wall from scrapes. The kit will do a 13-ft., 4-in. run. Panels are prefinished, offer four color/texture choices.

Put up a wainscot

Stop that drip

Even if you're used to it, there's no reason to subject company to the torture of a dripping faucet, not when a new washer is usually all that's needed. A conventional compression-type faucet is easy enough to take apart—but don't use pliers on the ribbed upper end of the valve stem. Turn off the water supply to the faucet first, of course. If you damage that ribbing, you may later be able to turn the handle with no trouble at all, but it won't operate the faucet. If you hold the stem in a vise to remove the washer bibb screw, it should be a wood-padded type for the same reason. If you've replaced the washer and the faucet still leaks, the seat needs attention, since a rough or badly worn seat can let water past even a new washer. Your hardware store should have a valve-seat grinding tool—just follow the instructions that come with it. Don't overdo it, and remember to rinse the cuttings out before you reassemble the faucet. If the leak persists after you've dressed the seat this way, it's time for a new seat (if it's replaceable) or a new faucet. To replace a seat, use an inexpensive seat wrench and coat the new seat's thread with pipe compound.

Tend to the toilet

If water continues to trickle into a toilet bowl after flushing, it probably means that the rubber stopper in the tank assembly has become hard with age and isn't making an effective seal. Shut off the water before making any toilet repairs. If the stopper is okay, or replacement doesn't help, the seat itself may be corroded, and cleaning it with emery cloth may be the answer.

Replacement of both stopper and seat with a modern flapper-type valve may be necessary, or you may have a worn washer in the float-valve assembly. With an old toilet, replacement of the entire float-and-valve assembly with a modern ballcock (without the float and arm) is a good idea.

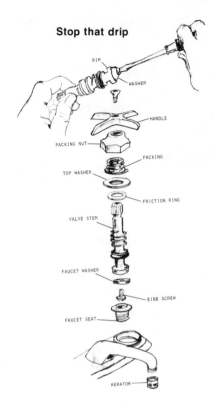

Stop that drip

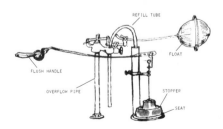

Tend to the toilet

Hide scratches

Blemishes (that's the trade term) on furniture—those small nicks and scratches—are easily dealt with. Just using a tinted polish on them may be enough. If that won't do it, use a touchup stick from your paint or hardware store. If you can't find one that's an exact color match, get two or more and blend them. Fill the scratch and rub well, then apply wax and rub that.

Hide scratches

Fix ceramic tile

Loose ceramic tile in the bathroom doesn't just look bad—it can lead to water damage. First, be sure to find *all* the loose tiles or you won't really be doing the job—tap with your fist, but not too hard, since you want to be able to put the original

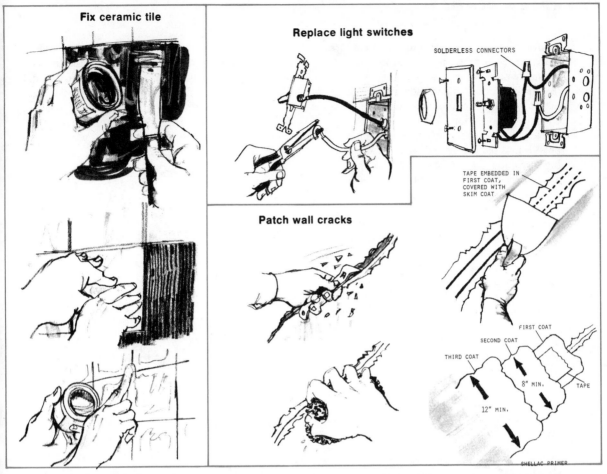

Fix ceramic tile

Replace light switches

SOLDERLESS CONNECTORS

Patch wall cracks

TAPE EMBEDDED IN
FIRST COAT,
COVERED WITH
SKIM COAT

FIRST COAT

SECOND COAT

THIRD COAT

8" MIN.

TAPE

12" MIN.

SHELLAC PRIMER

---

tile back up. With the tile down, scrape the old mastic off with a putty knife; you may have to soften it with solvent. Get the old grout off the tile; most you can break away, some you may have to grind or file off. Then apply new adhesive to the wall—be sure it's dry—as in the top picture, and spread it out with a serrated trowel.

Press the tiles into place, aligning them with others and allowing for grout lines. Acrylic latex grout is easiest to use. Press it into joints with a fingertip. Wipe down gently with a barely dampened sponge, then let the grout dry overnight before you rub with a soft, dry towel to take the white film off tile surfaces. To make tile sparkle, use a good glass cleaner.

Replace light switches

Here's how to fix that light switch in the guest room that hasn't worked right in years. Turn off the circuit at the service panel by yanking the fuse or flipping the circuit breaker. Remove switchplate and the screws that hold the old switch. Then it's no more than a matter of loosening the terminal screws on the old switch to remove the wires and then connecting the new switch.

See that the bare wire ends have a curl that's clockwise when they're in place, so they'll remain secure as you tighten terminal screws. Coil the wires back into the box and screw the new switch into place, taking care to align it for free operation with the switchplate replaced. If this is a job you don't like to do too often, put in a mercury switch; besides the advantage of silence, they also offer a service life of many years.

If the switch is in living room, dining room or family room (or any room used for TV watching), a dimmer switch is perfect for creating lighting moods (and saves electricity and lengthens a bulb life as well). Installation of a typical dimmer (for incandescent lighting in permanent fixtures) is shown above. Dimmer wires and supply wires are twisted together and solderless connectors (often supplied with the dimmer) are twisted on tightly; the dimmer is fastened to the box like an ordinary switch and the original switchplate replaced. Just be sure not to exceed specified wattage.

Patch wall cracks

To assure a good bond between patching compound and wall, the crack should be first Vgrooved (special tools are sold, but a can opener works perfectly well) then dusted so that no loose matter remains. Use a large sponge to dampen the crack thoroughly and then apply a first coat of the patching compound, forcing it into the crack with a 4-in. joint knife.

Press wallboard tape tightly into place, then press it into the compound with the knife, pressing hard enough to squeeze a little compound out at the edges. Cover tape with a thin skim coat. Three coats in all are recommended. Let each dry thoroughly and sand high spots down between coats (sand with care on plasterboard or you may damage paper surface). When the top coat is dry (after at least 24 hours), it can be feathered into adjoining surfaces by rubbing with a slightly dampened sponge. Easy does it, though, or you'll be rubbing the water-soluble compound off.

After the patch has been sponge-sanded, it must be primed or it will show through paint. White shellac is commonly used, but vinyl and oil-base primer-sealers are also suitable. Paint or wallcovering can then follow.

Replace ceiling tile

Ceiling tiles are up where you wouldn't expect them to get broken, but it does happen. You remove damaged tile by carefully cutting it out with a heavy utility knife, a jab saw (a short hacksaw blade with a handle at one end) or a keyhole saw. Clear the area in the frame of staples and bits of tile. To fit the hole, the replacement tile must be trimmed of protruding tongues—a utility knife should do the job. Apply adhesive (the type used with ceiling tile) to the back of the tile and press it into place, level with the surrounding tiles.

Resetting floor tile

Floor tiles that have lifted or curled up at edges or corners are a safety hazard as well as an eyesore. Apply a household iron, not to flatten them down, but to soften the old mastic below enough to let you lift each tile out. Then you scrape away as much as possible of the old adhesive and apply new. Press the tile back into place, wipe up excess mastic, and keep the tile under weights overnight.

Caulking bathtub seam

The crack that develops along the rim of the tub is easy to fix with modern caulks. First, make sure you remove *all* the old caulking, gouging it out with a stiff putty knife but taking care not to damage either tub or wall tiles. After dusting the cleaned seam, wipe it with alcohol to remove res-

idues that could keep the caulking from adhering. Caulking—a type specifically made for bath use—goes on in an unbroken bead just wider than the crack. Push it *into* the crack with a cloth or wet fingertip, forming a smooth, concave seam. A wet cloth will remove any excess caulking from the tile and tub.

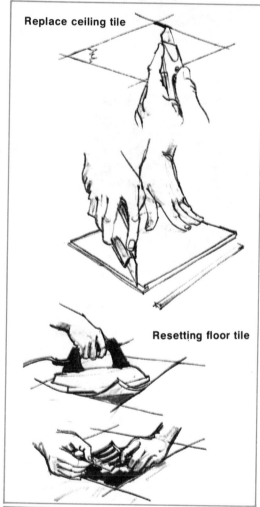

Replace ceiling tile

Resetting floor tile

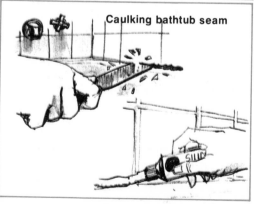

Caulking bathtub seam

These next four home-furnishing projects help you make the most of your living space. Following are plans and how-to tips on making the items.

Before the projects are assembled, fill all exposed edges of the plywood with wood filler. Then sand all parts with 100- or 120-grit abrasive paper. To assemble the projects, glue mating surfaces together. Then drive and set nails to hold the work while the glue dries.

Triangular storage table

Besides providing storage space and a display surface, this triangular table serves as a back-up for a sofa. The table is topped by a platform supported by recessed cleats to give the visual effect of a floating top.

Study the drawing of the table, and cut the table sides, noting the edges that receive a 45° bevel. Notice that one end of each shelf is cut at a

SIZED TO SOFA height, the triangular table provides a surface to display favorite objects and satisfy storage needs.

STORAGE TABLE

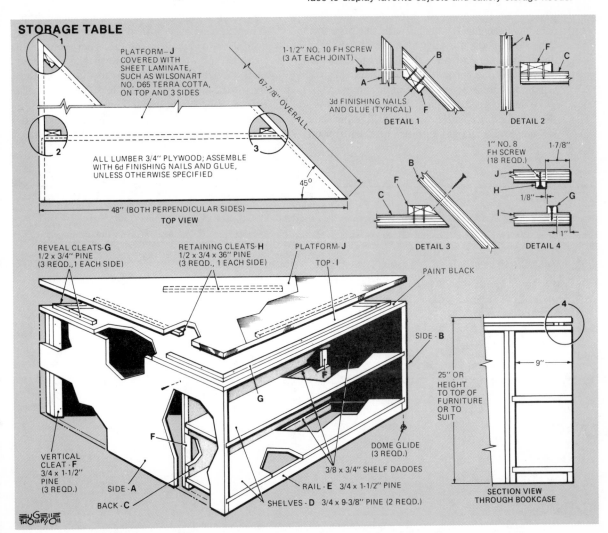

PLATFORM–J COVERED WITH SHEET LAMINATE, SUCH AS WILSONART NO. D65 TERRA COTTA, ON TOP AND 3 SIDES

67-7/8" OVERALL

ALL LUMBER 3/4" PLYWOOD; ASSEMBLE WITH 6d FINISHING NAILS AND GLUE, UNLESS OTHERWISE SPECIFIED

48" (BOTH PERPENDICULAR SIDES)

45°

TOP VIEW

1-1/2" NO. 10 FH SCREW (3 AT EACH JOINT)

3d FINISHING NAILS AND GLUE (TYPICAL)

DETAIL 1

DETAIL 2

DETAIL 3

1" NO. 8 FH SCREW (18 REQD.)

1-7/8"

1/8"

1"

DETAIL 4

REVEAL CLEATS-G 1/2 x 3/4" PINE (3 REQD.,1 EACH SIDE)

RETAINING CLEATS-H 1/2 x 3/4 x 36" PINE (3 REQD., 1 EACH SIDE)

PLATFORM-J

TOP - I

PAINT BLACK

SIDE - B

25" OR HEIGHT TO TOP OF FURNITURE OR TO SUIT

9"

G

VERTICAL CLEAT - F 3/4 x 1-1/2" PINE (3 REQD.)

F

SIDE - A

BACK - C

DOME GLIDE (3 REQD.)

3/8 x 3/4" SHELF DADOES

RAIL - E   3/4 x 1-1/2" PINE

SHELVES - D   3/4 x 9-3/8" PINE (2 REQD.)

SECTION VIEW THROUGH BOOKCASE

45° angle. Plow dadoes in the table sides and shelf back to receive the shelves.

Join the sides with three vertical cleats; two of the cleats have beveled sides (see drawing details Nos. 1 and 3). After assembling the sides, shelves, rail and top, let the unit dry overnight.

In a well-ventilated room, away from cigarets, sparks and open flames, cover platform J with plastic laminate. Laminate the platform edges first, one at a time. Laminate the top after trimming edges with a router and straight carbide cutter.

Cut the laminate at least ¼-in. wider and longer than the surface to be covered. Apply the adhesive evenly to the laminate with a short-nap (mohair) paint roller or bristle brush; then coat the wood surface. When you can touch brown paper to the surface without it sticking, the adhesive is ready for bonding, usually in 20 to 30 minutes.

Place clean wood strips, dowels or brown Kraft paper over the plywood. Lower the laminate carefully, keeping it aligned with the plywood. When the pieces are aligned, slide out the first dowel or paper and press the laminate onto the plywood at one corner. Continue removing the separators and pressing the laminate in place.

To ensure good bonding, apply pressure over the entire surface with a wooden rolling pin. Use a router and a straight carbide cutter to trim off the overhanging waste material. Make sure the plywood edge that the router follows is straight. If any voids are present, fill them with wood filler and sand the spots smooth. Otherwise, the router will follow the irregularities and miscut the laminate.

Bevel all corner edges with a 22½° carbide cutter in a router, or use a plane with a sharp blade set for scant removal. Smooth edges with a file, applying pressure only on the downstroke. Remove excess contact cement with lacquer thinner. Attach retaining-spacer cleats to the platform.

Paint the rest of the table. First prime the plywood with a pigmented shellac. Let it dry overnight, then paint with an alkyd or latex paint.

Position the platform on the table. The retaining cleats under the platform should fit within the reveal cleats on the tabletop.

Cube coffee table

You can build this cube table in a single shop session and finish it with plastic laminate. This piece serves as a coffee, end or corner table.

Cut the plywood sides and top and the pine cleats to size, as shown. Fill any holes in the edges with a quality wood filler. Then sand all surfaces smooth and brush them off.

Begin assembly by gluing and nailing one cleat to each side. Position the cleats as shown in the

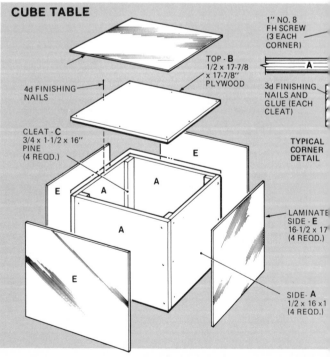

CUBE TABLE

1" NO. 8 FH SCREW (3 EACH CORNER)

TOP - **B** 1/2 x 17-7/8 x 17-7/8" PLYWOOD

4d FINISHING NAILS

3d FINISHING NAILS AND GLUE (EACH CLEAT)

CLEAT - **C** 3/4 x 1-1/2 x 16" PINE (4 REQD.)

TYPICAL CORNER DETAIL

LAMINATE SIDE - **E** 16-1/2 x 17 (4 REQD.)

SIDE - **A** 1/2 x 16 x1 (4 REQD.)

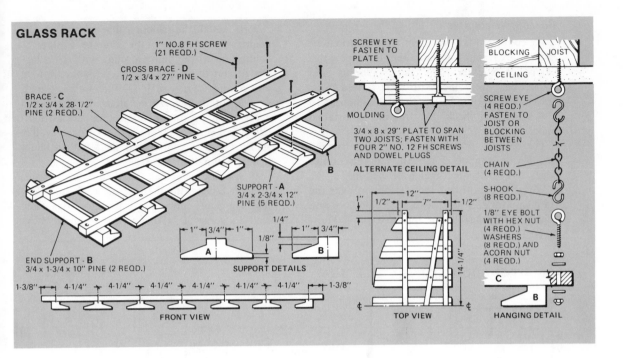

GLASS RACK

1" NO.8 FH SCREW (21 REQD.)

CROSS BRACE - D
1/2 x 3/4 x 27" PINE

BRACE - C
1/2 x 3/4 x 28-1/2"
PINE (2 REQD.)

A

B

END SUPPORT - B
3/4 x 1-3/4 x 10" PINE (2 REQD.)

SUPPORT - A
3/4 x 2-3/4 x 12"
PINE (5 REQD.)

SCREW EYE
FASTEN TO
PLATE

MOLDING

3/4 x 8 x 29" PLATE TO SPAN
TWO JOISTS; FASTEN WITH
FOUR 2" NO. 12 FH SCREWS
AND DOWEL PLUGS

ALTERNATE CEILING DETAIL

BLOCKING   JOIST

CEILING

SCREW EYE
(4 REQD.)
FASTEN TO
JOIST OR
BLOCKING
BETWEEN
JOISTS

CHAIN
(4 REQD.)

S-HOOK
(8 REQD.)

1/8" EYE BOLT
WITH HEX NUT
(4 REQD.)
WASHERS
(8 REQD.) AND
ACORN NUT
(4 REQD.)

C

B

HANGING DETAIL

1" 3/4" 1"
1/8"
A

1" 3/4"
B

SUPPORT DETAILS

1-3/8" 4-1/4" 4-1/4" 4-1/4" 4-1/4" 4-1/4" 4-1/4" 1-3/8"

FRONT VIEW

1"
1/2" 12" 7" 1/2"

14-1/4"

TOP VIEW

drawing. When nailing, drive and set all nails and fill the holes with wood filler. Then join the corners with glue and screws. Finally, glue and nail the top in place.

Make sure all edges are smooth before laminating.

Hanging glass rack

This overhead stemware rack has a "sculptured" look that is achieved by using your table saw. Begin by cutting the seven supports for the glasses and the three cross braces to length.

Set the table-saw blade to a ¼-in. elevation and the fence 1 in. from the blade to make the vertical cuts for each support. Then reset the table-saw blade at approximately a 20° angle and relocate the fence about ⅞ in. away on the other side of the blade. Test-cut in scrap wood, then turn the support on edge to cut out the waste.

Locate and bore screw and eyebolt holes in the braces on a drill press or with a portable drill.

Before assembly, sand parts smooth with 100-, then 120-grit abrasive paper; dust and wipe with a tack cloth. Space the supports, position the braces and mark the screw position on the braces. Then attach the supports to the braces. Mark the endpieces and cut them to length, using a band saw to create the "rounded" look on one side of the rack (see "top view" in the drawing).

Hang the rack temporarily, and brush on a primer. Follow this with coats of alkyd or latex

KEEP STEMWARE readily at hand—where it belongs logically—installed on the ceiling, directly over the service bar.

YOU CAN USE WASTED space for this bar/buffet unit for a family room.

paint to match decor. Allow adequate drying time between coats.

To install the rack, see the detail drawings.

Bar/buffet counter

We converted lally columns from obstructions to assets by framing around them to support this bar/buffet counter. The lally columns and counter base are framed with 2×3s, spaced 16 in. on center and assembled with 8d common nails. Use a level to check that framing is installed plumb.

The counter is a hollow-core door, covered with plastic laminate. First, laminate the counter edges, one at a time; then cover the top.

We used prefinished ¼-in. paneling over the framing. Mark all stud locations on the floor and ceiling before installing panels, so you'll know where to nail.

First, install the paneling that will adjoin the counter on the inside of the columns. Fasten the countertop to the column studs with 3-in. lag-screws and finish paneling the column framing and counter base. Use 3d (1¼ in.) finishing nails or 1-in. brads every 6 in. along the edges and every 12 in. on intermediate studs. Set all nail-heads and conceal them with special crayon-like sticks. Or, use color-coated nails with a slight head. Such nails aren't set.

If you use panel adhesive, use fewer nails. Squeeze a bead of adhesive onto each stud face; nail the panel along the top edge only. Then wedge a scrap of 2x3 between the panel bottom

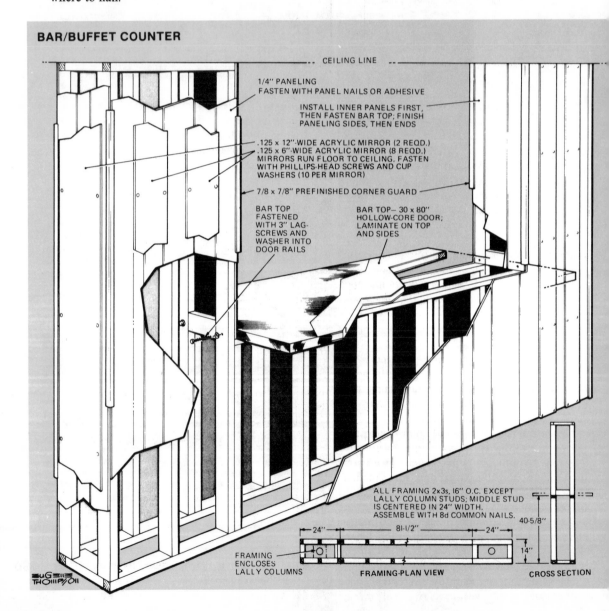

BAR/BUFFET COUNTER

CEILING LINE

1/4" PANELING
FASTEN WITH PANEL NAILS OR ADHESIVE

INSTALL INNER PANELS FIRST,
THEN FASTEN BAR TOP; FINISH
PANELING SIDES, THEN ENDS

.125 x 12"-WIDE ACRYLIC MIRROR (2 REQD.)
.125 x 6"-WIDE ACRYLIC MIRROR (8 REQD.)
MIRRORS RUN FLOOR TO CEILING. FASTEN
WITH PHILLIPS-HEAD SCREWS AND CUP
WASHERS (10 PER MIRROR)

7/8 x 7/8" PREFINISHED CORNER GUARD

BAR TOP
FASTENED
WITH 3" LAG-
SCREWS AND
WASHER INTO
DOOR RAILS

BAR TOP— 30 x 80"
HOLLOW-CORE DOOR;
LAMINATE ON TOP
AND SIDES

ALL FRAMING 2x3s, 16" O.C. EXCEPT
LALLY COLUMN STUDS; MIDDLE STUD
IS CENTERED IN 24" WIDTH.
ASSEMBLE WITH 8d COMMON NAILS.

40-5/8"

FRAMING
ENCLOSES
LALLY COLUMNS

24"   81-1/2"   24"

14"

FRAMING-PLAN VIEW

CROSS SECTION

and the studs to "air" the adhesive. After five minutes, remove the scrap wood and nail the panel to the studs.

Use prefinished corner guard to cover the paneling edges at the outside corners. If you use wooden corner guard, set the nailheads and conceal them with filler. Use only color-coated nails with vinyl corner guard.

To attach strips of mirrored sheet acrylic, bore oversize holes in each corner and center holes near the edge of each side of the strip. Secure acrylic to paneling with Phillips-head screws and cup washers.

Decorative planter

Greenery does wonders in adding a glamorous look to a bathroom. If you are looking for an attractive way to display plants, here's how it can be done cleverly with a cantilevered planter that actually does double duty in supporting the sink. Securely lagscrewed to studs in both back and end walls, an open frame as shown below will give ample support for the lavatory while providing flanking twin planters for live or artificial greens. If artificial, omit the metal liners and use 2-inch-thick slabs of green Styrofoam to hold your greenery. In each case, the planters are fitted with wood bottoms. You can make the box-like frame from common ¾-in. fir plywood and

give it a rich, expensive look by covering it with wood-grain plastic laminate. Use glue and flathead wood screws to assemble the frame. Fancy towel rings add to the overall good looks.

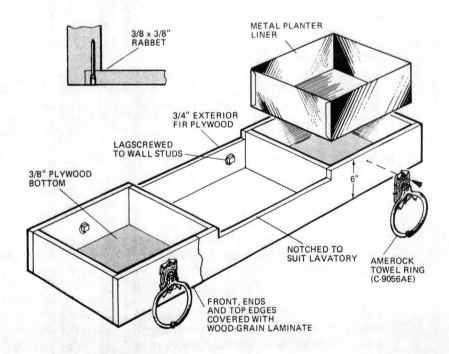

3/8 x 3/8" RABBET

METAL PLANTER LINER

3/4" EXTERIOR FIR PLYWOOD

LAGSCREWED TO WALL STUDS

3/8" PLYWOOD BOTTOM

6"

NOTCHED TO SUIT LAVATORY

AMEROCK TOWEL RING (C-9056AE)

FRONT, ENDS AND TOP EDGES COVERED WITH WOOD-GRAIN LAMINATE

LAUNDRY CENTER

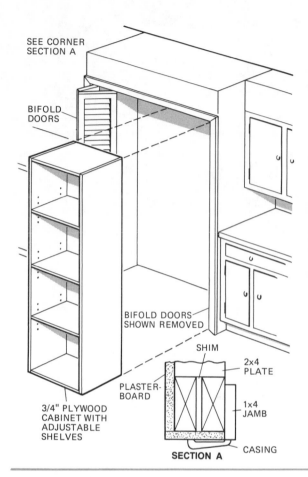

SEE CORNER
SECTION A

BIFOLD
DOORS

BIFOLD DOORS
SHOWN REMOVED

3/4" PLYWOOD
CABINET WITH
ADJUSTABLE
SHELVES

SHIM

2x4
PLATE

PLASTER-
BOARD

1x4
JAMB

CASING

SECTION A

Laundry center

When the wash is done and you'd like to park your rollabout compact washer out of sight, you can do it in this kitchen "garage." The built-in not only accommodates the washer and companion dryer but provides four roomy shelves for storage. When closed, good-looking bifold doors hide it all from view. A space-saver stack rack

HOME SECURITY

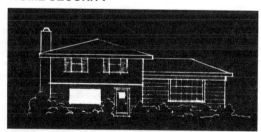

10:00 P.M. Kids in bed. Mom and Dad watch late movie in family room. Rest of house is dark.

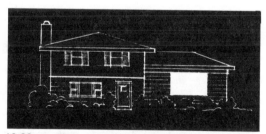

12:30 A.M. Movie is over, lights go out in family room, on in kitchen where Dad has midnight snack.

12:55 P.M. Snack's over, lights go out in kitchen, on in bedroom. Mom and Dad are retiring.

1:30 P.M. Junior awakens, makes trip to bathroom, leaves light on for Dad to turn out later.

lets you roll and store the washer under the dryer in a 21-in. space. The floor-to-ceiling, closet-like enclosure is framed with 2 x 4 studs and ⅜-in. plasterboard, and the freestanding shelf unit is a simple plywood box open front and back.

Door chime

If you have been wanting to update that raucous door buzzer with a new melodious chime but haven't done so because the thought of electricity bothers you, there's no need to worry. In making the switch from old to new, you are actually dealing with low-voltage wiring that's safe and easy to handle. The job requires little more than unhooking the existing wires and attaching your new chime. The diagram shows how wires from the front and back-door buttons go.

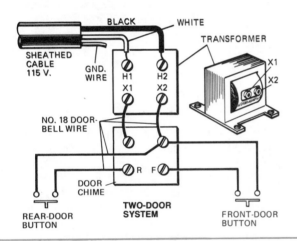

DOOR CHIMES can be contemporary works of art and striking wall accents.

Home security

Whether you're away on vacation or just out for the evening, lamps plugged into several automatic timers to go on and off at varying intervals in different rooms will give your home that "someone's-at-home" look and keep would-be intruders guessing. The price of three or four low-cost timers is a small investment toward safeguarding your home. Set to provide a normal lighting pattern around the clock, such timers will help make your home look occupied when it isn't. You can buy automatic timers where appliances are sold.

CONTROL TIMER plugs into wall outlet, lamp into timer. This unit turns lamp on/off at preset times on 24-hr. repeat cycle.

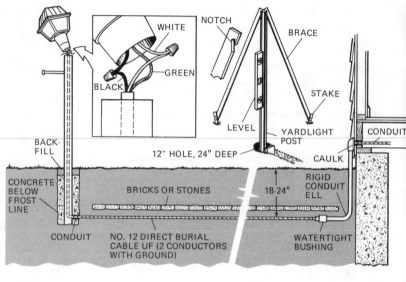

Lamppost for your yard

A yard light does many things. It bids welcome. It discourages prowlers. It adds nighttime beauty to the yard and lights the way to your door.

Before installing a yard light, check your local building department on electrical code compliance. Then dig a posthole (below the area's frostline) and a narrow trench to the power source. Once the cable is laid in the trench and up through the post, place the post in the hole, plumb and brace it in both planes with stakes.

Fill hole with concrete mix to about 6 in. below ground level. Let the concrete set 24 to 48 hours, then mount the lamp fixture. Attach the black cable wire to the black fixture wire, the white cable wire to the white fixture wire and the green cable wire to a ground connection on the fixture. If power is from a surface outlet on the house exterior, turn off the current and attach an L-shaped conduit to the outlet. Pull cable through the conduit and connect it. If no outside outlet is available, run conduit through the basement wall.

Dimmer switch

If dining by soft, simulated candlelight is not reason enough to install a dimmer control in place of the conventional toggle switch, maybe a lower electric bill is. Keeping lights in the TV room, baby's room and halls at a low level will save energy and money, even extend bulb life.

Some dimmers control light intensity by a knob you turn; others like this solid-state have a knob you slide up and down. It's simple to install a dimmer switch. Turn off the electricity, then remove screws holding the wall plate, back out the screws that hold the old switch in the outlet box and disconnect wires. Then reverse the steps to connect the new switch, press a fingertip control button in place over the end and turn the electricity back on.

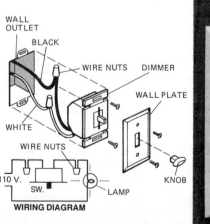

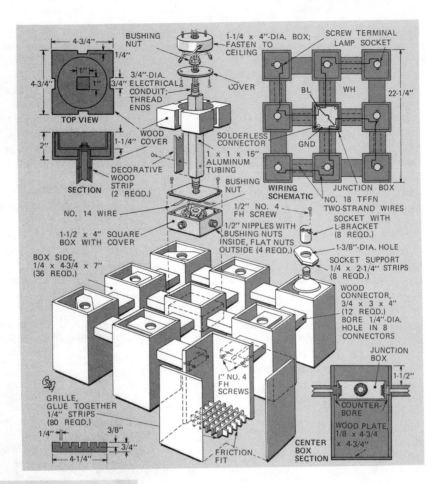

Contemporary light fixture

This teak fixture consists of eight light boxes surrounding a ninth box which holds an electrical junction box. Holes bored in wood connectors contain the wiring.

The wood parts consist of: nine wood boxes; 12 wood connectors with ¼-in-dia. holes through eight of them; eight socket supports, each with a center hole for a lamp socket. The egg-crate grilles are strips of wood, slot-joined and glued together, then friction-fitted in place. A decorative wood cover at the ceiling encloses the upper electrical box; use a router to make the hole for the box. This cover is held at the ceiling by two decorative wood strips attached to do-it-yourself aluminum tubing with screws.

Lay out box parts and wood connectors. Prebore screw holes in 12 connectors, ½-in. on center (o.c.) from each side, centered top to bottom; prebore screw holes in the box sides, 1⅜-in. o.c. from each side, and 1⅞-in. o.c. from top.

Next, glue the box parts together, except for

the center wood box. For strong joints, glue box sides around a wood form shielded with wax paper, consisting of two wood blocks whose dimensions equal the inside dimensions of the light boxes. Clamp the assembly with web clamp or rope.

Before assembling the wood box at center around the junction box, counterbore for the nipples and nuts; also bore and attach the four wood-block connectors that adjoin this box with glue and screws. Install the junction box; glue and clamp the wood sides with a web clamp around the junction box area. Glue the bottom plate. (Note: For extra strength, double these four connectors.)

Join the four light boxes to the connectors already attached to the center box, using a stubby screwdriver. Attach remaining connectors and corner boxes.

Install each socket support ½ in. down from the top of each box with glue and brads. Install the sockets. Then wire the fixture with No. 18 two-strand TFFN (Thermoplastic Fixture Flexible Nylon) wire from the junction box. At the junction box, join fixture wire to No. 14 wire and secure with solderless connectors; fasten ground wire to its screw.

Bore a center hole in the junction box cover. Secure the conduit to the box cover with a bushing nut. Run No. 14 wire through this conduit, then screw the cover to the junction box. Bore

VINYL-TAPE GRAPHIC adds visual impact to this bedroom. Tape comes sandwiched between paper. Remove the paper from the adhesive side, press tape to wall and peel off the top paper as shown.

screw holes for the teak-strip attaching screws in the aluminum tubing and get some assistance to install the whole fixture. First slip the aluminum tubing over the conduit, then the wood cover over the tubing. Attach conduit to the upper electrical box cover with a bushing nut and connect wires with solderless connectors. Then screw the box cover to the box. Slip the wood cover in place and secure the supporting wood strips. Install low-wattage lamps and grilles.

Tape wall graphic

An easy, inexpensive way to perk up a room is with tape stripes—the same type used on vans and four-wheel-drive vehicles. Automotive paint stores often stock these bright, multicolored stripes.

The graphic in this attic bedroom was made with a 50-ft. roll of a 10-in. wide, tricolor stripe. Installation took an hour.

The tape is double-backed. Peel away the paper protecting the adhesive side, lay the stripe

POT-AND-PAN rack holds kitchen utensils at hand. Traditionally, the movable rail hooks are used in the meat-packing industry.

in place, and rub the outer protective paper with a supplied nylon squeegee. The tape successfully covers textured walls. Angled bends other than 90° present a problem. However, if they're only slightly more or less, you *can* lap pieces of tape.

Pot-and-pan rack

This pot-and-pan rack is made of fir. Round the top corners of the 2x4 with a block plane and sandpaper. Locate the wall studs (probably 16 in. on center) and secure the 5-ft. spacer (2x2) to three studs, countersinking the screws. Space the screws, attaching the 2x4 to the spacer evenly. Countersink the screws and plug the holes with dowels. Stain the rack; finish with semigloss polyurethane.

You can make the rail hooks of ⅜-in.-dia. do-it-yourself aluminum rod. Cut a 12-in. length and mark bends (see drawing). Make a rod holder of two pieces of ¾×¾×3-in. hardwood, clamped into a ¾×1½×3 in. block. Bore a ⅜-in.-dia. hole centered on mating surfaces of blocks through shortest dimension. Then secure blocks between vise jaws. Insert the rod with the 2¼-in. section centered. Tighten the jaws *firmly*. Slip an 8-in. length of ½-in.-dia. iron pipe over the rod until the pipe end aligns at the first bend mark; lift up on the pipe to bend. Then make the second bend. Use the bending jig shown in the drawing to make the third bend. Cut off waste *after* making the bends.

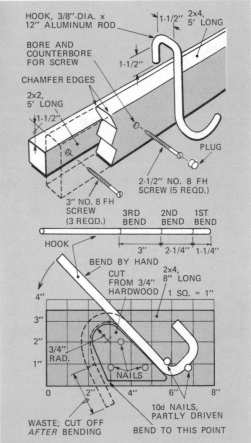

Strips of wood create an unusual room

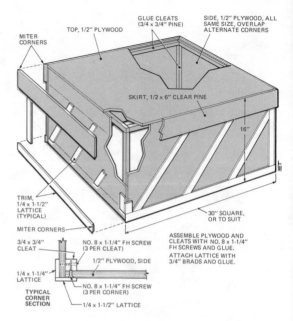

GLUE CLEATS (3/4 x 3/4" PINE)

SIDE, 1/2" PLYWOOD, ALL SAME SIZE, OVERLAP ALTERNATE CORNERS

TOP, 1/2" PLYWOOD

MITER CORNERS

SKIRT, 1/2 x 6" CLEAR PINE

16"

TRIM, 1/4 x 1-1/2" LATTICE (TYPICAL)

MITER CORNERS

30" SQUARE, OR TO SUIT

3/4 x 3/4" CLEAT

NO. 8 x 1-1/4" FH SCREW (3 PER CLEAT)

1/2" PLYWOOD, SIDE

1/4 x 1-1/4" LATTICE

NO. 8 x 1-1/4" FH SCREW (3 PER CORNER)

TYPICAL CORNER SECTION

1/4 x 1-1/2" LATTICE

ASSEMBLE PLYWOOD AND CLEATS WITH NO. 8 x 1-1/4" FH SCREWS AND GLUE. ATTACH LATTICE WITH 3/4" BRADS AND GLUE.

■ INSTALLING LATTICE STRIPS over a painted wall is one quick way to give a room a new feeling. And, if you can apply strips to one or more pieces of furniture at the same time, you will give the room a custom look.

In the room shown, strips of 1½-in.-wide lattice are applied diagonally to the wall at 45° angles. The vertical and horizontal strips that box in the diagonals simplify the installation considerably.

The coffee table is a shop project that requires one sheet of ½-in. plywood and about a weekend of your time. You can use interior-grade, A-D plywood for the table and not worry about the edges because they will be covered with lattice.

All four sides are exactly the same size. Cut these pieces first when building the table; then carefully stack them to make sure they are identical.

On the D side of the plywood, install the glue cleats at one end of each side as shown—set back ½ in. to receive the joining side. The cleats can be fastened using either 1¼-in. ringed nails or 1-in. flathead screws (turned into countersunk holes.) If you opt for the nails, use your diagonal cutter to nip off the tip of each nail before driving (or the points will come through the plywood). Next, install the cleats upon which the top will rest. With sides completed, the case can be assembled.

When all four sides are assembled, check with a square to make certain corners are exactly 90°. *Before the glue has a chance to dry,* measure for, and cut, the top piece. Install the top using glue and flathead screws in *deep* countersunk holes. If you have cut the top perfectly square and with a neat fit, it will hold the case square while the glue dries. When dry, the screw holes on top can be filled.

Lay out the lattice and cut all strips and assemble without glue to check for layout and fit. When satisfied, remove the lattice and apply a finish before final assembly.

For a proper finish, sand all surfaces of the table with a belt sander; first use an 80-grit paper, then 120-grit. Dust off and apply a coat of a pigmented shellac. Repeat the steps for the lattice.

Next, sand all painted surfaces lightly with 150-grit abrasive paper; dust and wipe with a tack cloth. Apply the finish color of your choice to the table and semigloss paint to the lattice.

Lattice for the walls should also be painted before application. It can be secured to the wall using flathead wood screws into wall studs or white glue and 6d finishing nails. No matter which fastener you use, be sure to predrill holes to avoid splitting.

WHILE THIS coffee table can be sized to fit the space you plan to put it in, construction method remains the same. Cut parts and test-assemble them, then disassemble and paint. Lattice on walls can be screwed or nailed.

Let the sun shine in

■ THE ENCLOSED PORCH in these pictures was added onto a house, and although there are windows all along the outside wall, little light was transmitted across the porch into the adjacent living room. Dark wood on walls and ceilings made the porch seem smaller than it really was.

A dormer or a raised roof might have worked here. But of all possibilities, a skylight was the easiest and least expensive.

ONE BIG skylight turned this enclosed porch into a solarium that is bright on the dreariest days. At night you can stay warm while you count the stars

The ceiling was opened with the largest skylight available, a 46-inch-square unit. It comes fully assembled and framed, uses integral copper flashing, and has a screen and an operator mechanism to lift the bubble for summer venting. This type is less susceptible than a fixed unit to condensation caused by hot, humid air collecting near the ceiling. For a vaulted ceiling or crawlspace over a flat ceiling, the roof installation is the same. A dropped ceiling needs more framing to close off the crawlspace.

To start, locate the skylight area inside and make corresponding measurements to get the exact location on the roof. On a vaulted ceiling, after cutting away the drywall, drive a 10d nail up through the roof at each corner of the opening to mark the cutout. With the area outlined, pull off shingles and felt paper and cut through the roof deck with a sabre saw. Then cut away the center rafter. Be sure to cut an extra 3 inches at each end to allow for double headers that frame the opening and carry the load from the interrupted rafter. Repeat this cut in the wooden ceiling below but increase the depth of the opening to let in more light. Then nail 2×4 uprights along edges of the two openings to frame the short tunnel between outer and inner roofs.

To make the new installation more waterproof, set flashing around the unit in a bed of roof cement and secure the bubble with nails through the frame into the adjacent rafters. The final step outside is to lace the shingles (use the ones you removed) back into the roofing pattern and cut them to fit the flashing. Above the unit you set the shingles on a second bed of cement over the copper flange to prevent water from backing up underneath. Along sides, shingles should run 2 to 3 in. past the lip of the flashing that is secured to the roof with copper clips. On the lower edge, the

RAIN, ICE and snow don't bother the unit shown above. You can leave it open for ventilation and not run home to close it if it starts to rain. A curved flange at the base keeps water from dripping into the opening. The hardware is strong enough to break through a crust of ice after a storm (left). Check your job with a hose test (right).

TOOLS OF THE TRADE

HAMMER

NAIL PULLER

MAT KNIFE

SHINGLE SNIPS

POINTING TROWEL

CROSSCUT SAW

SQUARE

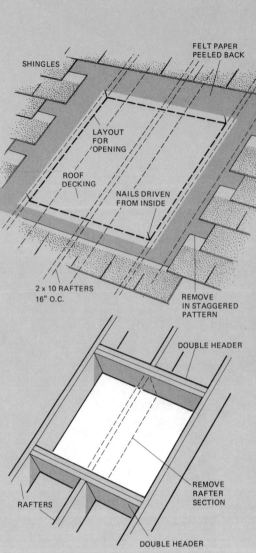

SHINGLES

FELT PAPER PEELED BACK

LAYOUT FOR OPENING

ROOF DECKING

NAILS DRIVEN FROM INSIDE

2 x 10 RAFTERS 16" O.C.

REMOVE IN STAGGERED PATTERN

DOUBLE HEADER

RAFTERS

REMOVE RAFTER SECTION

DOUBLE HEADER

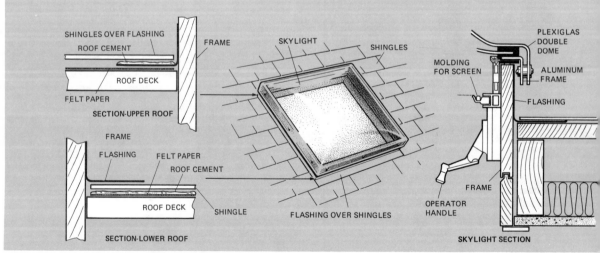

SHINGLES OVER FLASHING

ROOF CEMENT

FRAME

ROOF DECK

FELT PAPER

SECTION-UPPER ROOF

FRAME

FLASHING

FELT PAPER

ROOF CEMENT

ROOF DECK

SHINGLE

SECTION-LOWER ROOF

SKYLIGHT

SHINGLES

FLASHING OVER SHINGLES

PLEXIGLAS DOUBLE DOME

MOLDING FOR SCREEN

ALUMINUM FRAME

FLASHING

FRAME

OPERATOR HANDLE

SKYLIGHT SECTION

THE ROOF window shown above is made in Denmark.

flashing sits in a bed of roof cement spread on top of the shingles so all water will run onto the roof surface. While the frame is open, check the installation for leaks by simulating a downpour with a garden hose.

Use ¼-inch AC plywood over the tunnel frame and paint it white to reflect as much light as possible. Molding strips along edges of the ceiling cutout give a final finishing touch. You can treat the interior many ways (even with mirrors) but you must make the exterior waterproof. Follow the window maker's instructions and the steps outlined here. Pinpointing the source of a leak later on is, at best, a guessing game; you may have to redo all the flashing.

In the room shown here, the back wall of the tunnel was angled to let the sun's rays stream directly through double glass doors into the living room. The porch is now so bright that it has been converted into a solarium with plants.

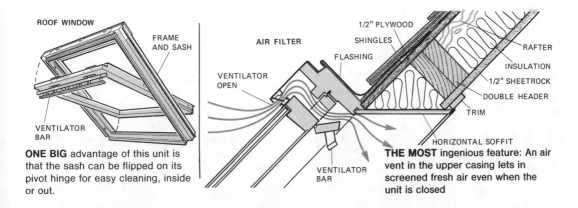

ROOF WINDOW

FRAME AND SASH

VENTILATOR BAR

ONE BIG advantage of this unit is that the sash can be flipped on its pivot hinge for easy cleaning, inside or out.

AIR FILTER

VENTILATOR OPEN

VENTILATOR BAR

1/2" PLYWOOD

SHINGLES

FLASHING

RAFTER

INSULATION

1/2" SHEETROCK

DOUBLE HEADER

TRIM

HORIZONTAL SOFFIT

THE MOST ingenious feature: An air vent in the upper casing lets in screened fresh air even when the unit is closed

Enlarge and facelift your kitchen

■ AMERICAN HOMEOWNERS are staying put and improving what they already own. For some, home improvement may mean adding a bedroom in the attic or basement. For others, a new family room may be needed. For many, there is a need to create a bigger kitchen and possibly an eat-in area in that room.

We enlarged the kitchen shown by knocking out a section of an exterior kitchen wall after relocating several appliances. We built new cabinets which matched the originals in the existing kitchen, thereby creating a smooth visual transition. And we covered the walls with rough-sawn planking and fitted the ceiling with false beams to achieve a country look.

AN OLD TABLE, simply freshened with glossy-finish latex-alkyd paint, makes a totally new dining center.

Adding a room

Once you've decided upon the location and size of your addition, you must determine whether the wall to be removed is a bearing wall (one which supports the load imposed by the roof). If you lack the know-how to determine joist run and how a roof is supported, play it safe: Call in a professional engineer for advice.

If it is a bearing wall, install a temporary wall, located about 1 ft. inside the house wall, to support the joists overhead during the tearing out and rebuilding. Use 2x4s for the plates and studs for the temporary wall, and drive shims beneath the bottom plate, if necessary, to assure the wall being wedged securely in place. The building codes and zoning laws in many communities require a permit before the building lines of a residence may be altered. So check with your local building department before you put a saw to the wall.

At this time, determine whether there are any water or heat pipes, or electrical wires in the wall. If there are, take every precaution to avoid damaging them during the rip-out operation. To be safe, turn off water to water pipes, electricity to electric lines, and so on before starting.

Locate your opening and use a large-diameter bit in your drill to mark the upper corners of the cutout. Next, go outside and pinpoint the interior floor elevation on the outside wall, using the holes to guide you.

Your footings and block wall (or slab) must be installed before you make the wall cutout—but first you must know the floor elevation.

Knocking out a wall

Remove the siding, then use your spirit level to mark the horizontal and vertical lines to be cut. Set your saw blade to cut to a depth of about ⅞ in. (standard siding thickness is ¾ in.) and make

the cut. *Caution:* Only an experienced saw user should make this type of wall cutout with a portable circular. There is a great possibility of kickback—especially when moving the saw overhead.

Take off the sheathing below, then remove the interior wall, in the same fashion. Finally, cut out the studs. Next, install the appropriate-size header and posts to support it. If it's not a bearing wall, you can use a pair of 2x6s, spiked together. If the wall carries weight from above, ask the local building department, or a professional engineer, to calculate the size header needed.

If you plan to build the addition yourself, you'd be wise to buy a good carpentry reference book.

Making an add-on work

There's an important design consideration when planning a house addition—how it will look both outside and inside. The shape of the add-on, plus the materials used for siding, roof, windows and so on should blend perfectly with what is already there. New windows should match the old in style and should be installed at

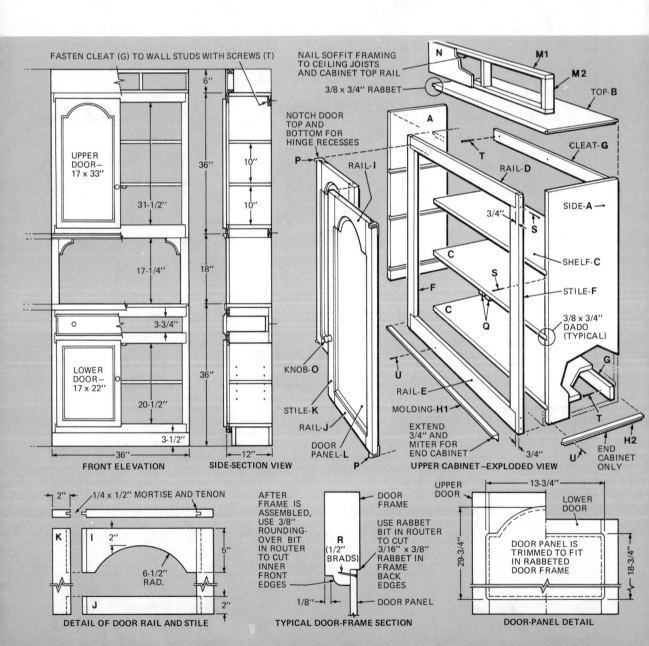

FASTEN CLEAT (G) TO WALL STUDS WITH SCREWS (T)

UPPER DOOR— 17 x 33"

LOWER DOOR— 17 x 22"

FRONT ELEVATION

SIDE-SECTION VIEW

NAIL SOFFIT FRAMING TO CEILING JOISTS AND CABINET TOP RAIL

3/8 x 3/4" RABBET

NOTCH DOOR TOP AND BOTTOM FOR HINGE RECESSES

RAIL-I

KNOB-O

STILE-K

RAIL-J

DOOR PANEL-L

TOP-B

CLEAT-G

RAIL-D

SIDE-A

SHELF-C

STILE-F

3/8 x 3/4" DADO (TYPICAL)

RAIL-E

MOLDING-H1

EXTEND 3/4" AND MITER FOR END CABINET

END CABINET ONLY

UPPER CABINET—EXPLODED VIEW

1/4 x 1/2" MORTISE AND TENON

6-1/2" RAD.

DETAIL OF DOOR RAIL AND STILE

AFTER FRAME IS ASSEMBLED, USE 3/8" ROUNDING-OVER BIT IN ROUTER TO CUT INNER FRONT EDGES

R (1/2" BRADS)

DOOR FRAME

USE RABBET BIT IN ROUTER TO CUT 3/16" x 3/8" RABBET IN FRAME BACK EDGES

DOOR PANEL

TYPICAL DOOR-FRAME SECTION

UPPER DOOR

LOWER DOOR

13-3/4"

29-3/4"

DOOR PANEL IS TRIMMED TO FIT IN RABBETED DOOR FRAME

18-3/4"

DOOR-PANEL DETAIL

the same elevation as the existing ones.

Inside, it's important to create a finished room that feels as though it has always been there. Color is an effective device here: A careful selection of paints and wallpapers can make an add-on compatible with any connected room.

This kitchen's walls were skinned with rough-sawn planking—brand-new stock from the lumberyard—which was coated with paint to achieve a barn-board effect. (Using solid wood on the walls also makes it easier to hang the new wall cabinets.)

The beams overhead are false (hollow), installed over furring strips that are nailed to the joist undersides.

Cupboard

As can be seen in the drawings, the cupboard is built in base- and wall-cabinet modules. No exotic woodworking techniques are used here; the cabinets are built using the straightforward methods employed in many cabinet shops.

Use white glue throughout for all joinery. Since you're working with pine stiles and rails,

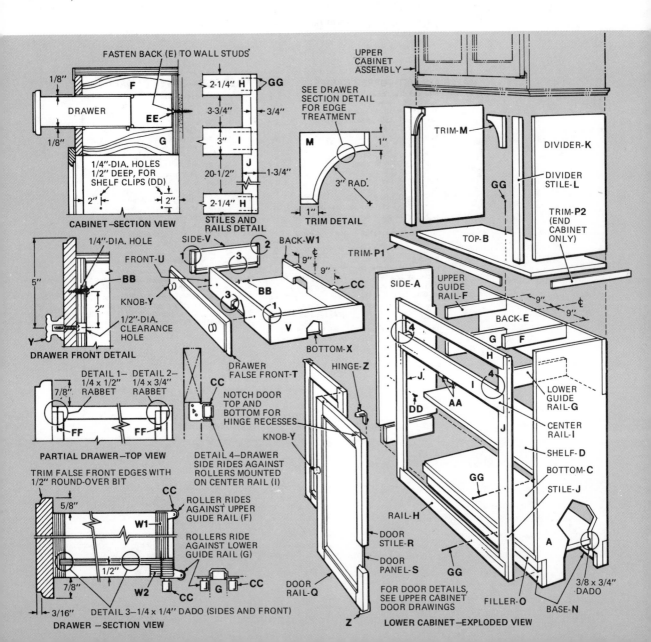

you can secure joints with 6d and 8d finishing nails. The nails should be set and hidden with wood filler. When nailing near a board end, pre-bore a head hole to avoid splitting the wood member.

We suggest you build the cabinets in your shop, then haul them to your new room for installation. Install the cabinets by securing them to wall cleats nailed to wall studs. Be absolutely certain that you build the cabinets in your run with a "scribe." A scribe is simply an over-wide outside stile. Thus, the stile that abuts the wall should be cut and installed on the cabinet so that it extends about 2 in. beyond the cabinet's side. This extra material can then be scribed to the wall, using a divider to ensure a perfect fit. If there's any gap between the end of the cabinet run and the wall, conceal with a narrow molding.

Painting the cabinets

Though it takes a little more time, it's better to paint the cabinets after they are up. This way, you can patch, sand and conceal any damage that may have occurred during their installation. To speed the job somewhat, however, apply the prime coat of paint while the cabinets are still in the shop.

Painting the two colors on the molding detail (bead shape on door fronts) takes both time and a steady hand.

These accent colors should be added after the cabinet has been painted and you have allowed ample time for it to dry.

To avoid wavy lines, use masking tape on both sides of the molding detail. Make certain that you press down the edge securely so the paint won't bleed underneath.

MATERIALS LIST—UPPER CABINET

Key	No.	Size and description (use)
A	2	3/4 × 11¼ × 36⅜" plywood (side)
B	1	3/4 × 11¼ × 36" plywood (top)
C	3	3/4 × 11¼ × 35¼" plywood (shelf)
D	1	3/4 × 2¼ x 34½" pine (rail)
E	1	3/4 × 3 × 34½" pine (rail)
F	2	3/4 × 1¾ × 36¾" pine (stile)
G	2	3/4 × 2¼ × 34½" pine (wall cleat)
H1	1	3/4 × ⅞ × 36" solid crown molding
H2	1	3/4 × ⅞ × 12¾" solid crown molding
I	2	3/4 × 5 × 14" pine (upper door rail)
J	2	3/4 × 2 × 14" pine (lower door rail)
K	4	3/4 × 2 × 33" pine (door stile)
L	2	¼ × 13¾ × 29¾" plywood (door panel)
M1	2	3/4 × 1½", length to suit, furring strips (soffit plates)
M2	*	3/4 × 1½", length to suit, furring strips (soffit studs)
N		½" drywall
O	2	1½"-dia. wooden knob
P	2 pr.	Vertical, stile-mounted pivot hinge for overlay door
Q	2	Magnetic catch
R	*	½" brad
S	*	8d finishing nail
T	*	3" No. 12 fh screw
U	*	2d finishing nail
Y	4	1½"-dia. wooden knob
Z		Two pair of vertical, stile-mounted pivot hinges for overlay door
AA	2	Magnetic catch
BB	2	1" No. 8 fh screw and washer
CC	2	Plastic roller set
DD	4	Shelf support clip
EE	3	3" No. 12 fh screw
FF	*	2d finishing nail
GG	*	8d finishing nail

*As required.

MATERIALS LIST—LOWER CABINET

Key	No.	Size and description (use)
A	2	3/4 × 11¼ × 35¼" plywood (side)
B	1	3/4 × 12 × 36" plywood (top)
C	1	3/4 × 11¼ × 35¼" plywood (bottom)
D	1	3/4 × 11 × 34" plywood (adjustable shelf)
E	1	3/4 × 9 × 36" plywood (rail)
F	2	3/4 × 2¼ × 10½" pine (upper guide rail)
G	2	3/4 × 3 × 10½" pine (lower guide rail)
H	2	3/4 × 2¼ × 34½" pine (face rail)
I	1	3/4 × 3 × 34½" pine (face rail)
J	2	3/4 × 1¾ × 32½" pine (stile)
K	2	3/4 × 11¼ × 17¼" plywood (divider)
L	2	3/4 × 2 × 17¼" pine (divider stile)
M	2	3/4 × 4 × 4" pine (trim)
N	2	3/4 × 5 × 36" plywood (base)
O	1	3/4 × 1½ × 36" pine (filler)
P1	1	¼ × 1⅜ × 36" pine lattice (trim)
P2	1	¼ × 1⅜ × 12¼" pine lattice (trim)
Q	4	3/4 × 2 × 14" pine (door rail)
R	4	3/4 × 2 × 22" pine (door stile)
S	2	⅛ × 13¾ × 18¾" plywood (door panel)
T	4	3/4 × 5 × 24" pine (drawer face)
U	1	½ × 3½ × 31¾" plywood (drawer front)
V	2	½ × 3½ × 9¾" plywood (drawer side)
W1	1	½ × 2¾ × 31¾" plywood (drawer back)
W2	2	½ × 1 × 3" pine (roller cleat)
X	1	¼ × 9½ × 31¾" plywood (drawer bottom)

Wainscoting

■ WAINSCOTING is a general term applied to many different wall treatments. Some traditional examples are: flat-panel wainscoting, which consists of a series of flat panels surrounded with rails and stiles, much like cabinet doors; raised-panel wainscoting, fabricated in a similar manner, but which is usually considered more elegant because of the time and effort required; and the double V-joint and bead wainscoting (shown here), which is probably the most prevalent. It's still available in open stock at many lumberyards and is usually made of pine or fir, sometimes in different grades. If you plan to paint it, as done here, you can save money by using the less expensive grade. In fact, your choice of wainscoting materials is by no means limited to these traditional examples.

Three basic ways to attach wainscoting

You need horizontal nailing for the boards at least every 24 in. This is required because the boards are narrow and applied vertically. The studs within the wall are aligned the same way, typically on 16-in. centers. Therefore, the voids between the wall studs have to be spanned to provide nailing surfaces for the wainscoting boards.

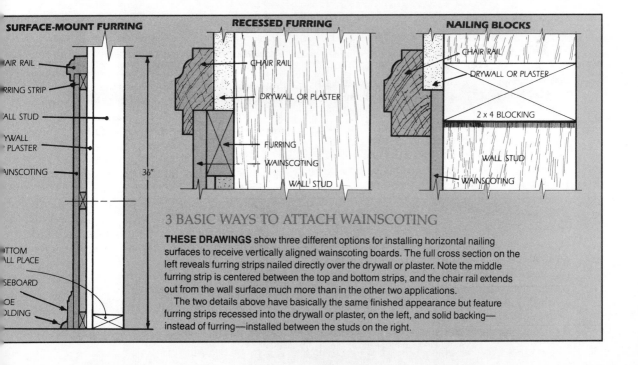

3 BASIC WAYS TO ATTACH WAINSCOTING

THESE DRAWINGS show three different options for installing horizontal nailing surfaces to receive vertically aligned wainscoting boards. The full cross section on the left reveals furring strips nailed directly over the drywall or plaster. Note the middle furring strip is centered between the top and bottom strips, and the chair rail extends out from the wall surface much more than in the other two applications.

The two details above have basically the same finished appearance but feature furring strips recessed into the drywall or plaster, on the left, and solid backing—instead of furring—installed between the studs on the right.

BEGIN BY ESTABLISHING HEIGHT of boards. Mark wall at this point, then draw a level line through mark and continue it around room, maintaining precise level as you go.

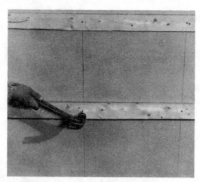

IF YOU DON'T HAVE HORIZONTAL BLOCKING between studs, nail furring strips directly onto surface to receive the wainscoting. Nail into every wall stud.

IF YOU'D RATHER RECESS THE FUR-RING, draw an outline around each strip and cut out the drywall behind with a utility knife. Then nail furring directly onto the studs.

START INSTALLING BOARDS at room corner or door casing as shown here. For pro results, use level to plumb first board in place. Mark plumb position for reference.

IF FIRST BOARD DOESN'T FIT tightly to casing or room corner when held in plumb position, scribe back edge to conform to irregularities. Then plane edge to meet line.

ONCE BOARD IS PLANED TO FIT, nail in place with finishing nails near back edge. The end boards are the only ones nailed through the surface. Set heads and fill nail holes.

Surface-mount furring

Probably the easiest way is to nail furring strips across the surface of the wall, hitting each wall stud with a nail. This method has one minor drawback. Because both the furring and the wainscoting are applied over the drywall or plaster, the finished surface extends at least 1 in. into the room, depending on the material you use—$^{11}/_{16}$ in. or ¾ in. for the furring and $^{5}/_{16}$ in. or ⅜ in. for the wainscoting.

Recessed furring

A second method gains some space because the furring is recessed into the drywall or plaster. To do this, just position the furring strips in their proper place on the wall, trace their outlines, then cut out the wall covering material behind. Nail the furring directly onto the studs. Of course, you can remove all the drywall or plaster, but this is time-consuming and messy.

Nailing blocks

If you do remove all the drywall or plaster, you have a third option that reduces the projection of the wainscoting to a minimum. This is to nail solid blocking between the studs, flush with the outside edge of the studs. Then nail the wainscoting directly across these framing members.

A variation of this method was used in our installation. The room had been gutted, solid blocking added between the studs, and new drywall installed on the walls and ceiling. We wanted the finished surface of the wainscoting boards to project the extra ½ in. into the room, so we installed the drywall over the lower part of the wall.

Installing the wainscoting boards

First, decide on what height you want your chair rail. We chose 36 in., which is fairly standard but by no means a rule.

Next, cut all the wainscoting boards to length using a radial-arm saw or a circular saw with a cutting jig. Start installation at a room corner or alongside a door casing. Plumb the first wainscoting board in place, scribe and plane it to fit flush, then nail it in place.

Keep in mind these boards have a tongue on one edge and a groove on the other. Because of this built-in joinery method, once the first board

is nailed soundly in place, all following boards are nailed only through the tongue. These nails will be hidden by the groove of the next board. You must work carefully when nailing so you don't split the tongue. Angle the nails at approximately 45 °.

For right-handed people, working left to right on the wall is generally more convenient. For left-handed people, the opposite direction is better.

ATTACH TONGUE EDGE of board by driving nail through corner where tongue and bead meet. Angle nail at approximately 45° and set head.

DRIVE NEXT BOARD INTO PLACE so groove fits over first board's tongue. Use scrap block of wainscoting to prevent damaging edge. Nail second board through tongue only.

IF BOARD IS SLIGHTLY WARPED, you can often pry it tight by driving a chisel into the wall or furring strip and pulling back on chisel. Hold in place while driving nail.

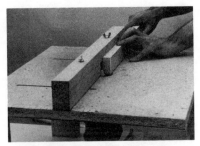

IF YOU WANT TO FABRICATE your own chair rail, use a router table to make the cuts. To duplicate our pattern, begin cutting the back rabbet with a straight cutter.

NEXT, CUT BOTTOM RABBET on board face, then turn board over and cut roman ogee shape near top. Don't cut full depth in one pass. Use two or three passes for a clean cut.

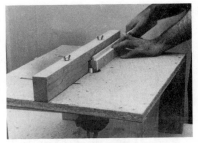

WHEN OGEE HAS BEEN CUT to depth shown in the drawing, install straight cutter in router and trim off waste below ogee to complete the finished shape.

LIGHTLY SAND RAIL to remove any sharp edges and you're done. Completed shape required only two cutters: roman ogee shown and straight cutter still in router.

When you come to an electrical outlet, turn off the power to that circuit at your fuse box or breaker box. Then remove the covering plate and the screws holding the receptacle in the wall box. Pull the receptacle away from the box, being careful not to damage any of the insulation on the wires. It is not necessary to remove the wires—you just need enough room to work around the receptacle.

Cut the board or boards so the perimeter of the box is just visible. Then nail the boards on the wall. Screw the receptacle back in place so its positioning ears, on the top and bottom, bear directly on the surface of the boards. Then attach the covering plate and turn on the power.

Installing the chair rail

Once all the boards are nailed on the wall, cut and install a chair rail of your choice. You can either buy a stock rail at a lumberyard or cut one of your own design on a shaper or a router table. The pattern is for the one shown in these illustrations.

Finish up by installing a baseboard at the floor and a shoe molding over it if you choose. Now you should sand the whole wall with 220-grit sandpaper, remove the dust and apply a finish of your choice. You could also sand each board after it is cut and before you nail it to the wall, saving you the discomfort of trying to sand a low, vertical surface.

CUTTING JIG FOR CIRCULAR SAW

WEAR SAFETY GOGGLES

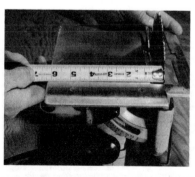 

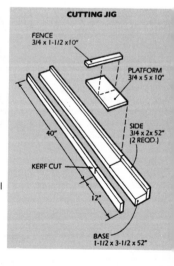

CUTTING JIG

FENCE
3/4 x 1-1/2 x10"

PLATFORM
3/4 x 5 x 10"

SIDE
3/4 x 2x 52"
(2 REQD.)

40"

KERF CUT

12"

BASE
1-1/2 x 3-1/2 x 52"

IF YOU'RE INSTALLING A LOT OF WAINSCOTING, you've got a lot of straight cuts to make, all the same length. A radial-arm saw is the ideal tool, but if you don't have one, this simple-to-build jig for a circular saw will save a lot of time. Assemble the parts as shown in the drawing above, making sure the fence is installed square to the sides. Then just slide the boards into the jig and make the cuts. Clamp a stop block at the far end of the jig so you won't have to measure each board.

Measure distance from side of shoe to saw blade, then install fence on jig so blade just clears end of saw platform. When parts are assembled, set blade to cut 1/8 in. into top of 2 x 4. Then make kerf cut, keeping shoe tight to fence.

Your house number belongs in lights

■ EVER WANDER DOWN a strange, dark street peering at invisible house numbers to find the address you're after? Your guests won't have that problem if you illuminate your house number—and you can do it without running new wiring.

The trick is a low-voltage lighting system that draws its power from your doorbell's transformer. This circuit is always on, and its wiring comes right out to the bell button, where it's easy to tap into. The bulbs are No. 49 "flea-power" types requiring only 60 thousandths of an ampere each, at two volts. Use five bulbs in series for a 10-volt bell circuit, eight in series for a 16-volt chime setup.

While the wiring to the doorbell button may appear to be only a switch loop, what you're actually doing is drawing power through the bell circuit—just enough to light the bulbs, but not enough to activate the bell. When the button is pressed, the light will momentarily go out and full power routed to the bell will ring it.

Choose a plastic box big enough to hold your house number. If its lid is transparent, make it translucent with a light spray of white acrylic paint to diffuse the light. The numbers can be plastic or metal.

The reflector assembly is cut from a 12-ounce, aluminized-cardboard frozen-juice can. The miniature bayonet sockets are bolted to the reflector as shown in the drawing.

Wire the bulbs in series and run the wire through a hole in the box; knot the wire inside so the connections won't loosen if the wire is yanked, and leave enough wire outside to reach the doorbell button.

The bolts that hold the reflector to the box, and the screws holding the box to the wall, should pass through washers and rubber grommets, so the box won't crack when you snug up the screws.

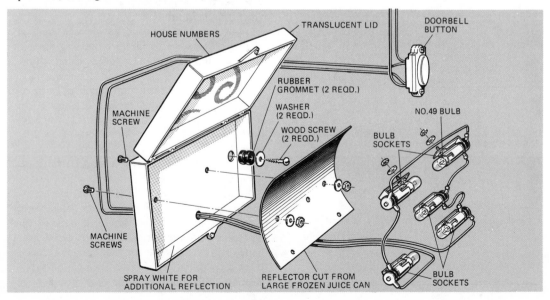

HOUSE NUMBERS
TRANSLUCENT LID
DOORBELL BUTTON
RUBBER GROMMET (2 REQD.)
MACHINE SCREW
WASHER (2 REQD.)
WOOD SCREW (2 REQD.)
NO.49 BULB
BULB SOCKETS
MACHINE SCREWS
SPRAY WHITE FOR ADDITIONAL REFLECTION
REFLECTOR CUT FROM LARGE FROZEN JUICE CAN
BULB SOCKETS

Mildew prevention

Moisture, mold and mildew

The drawings and dew point chart help explain when and why condensation occurs and moisture problems develop. Dewpoint is the temperature at which dew starts to form or vapor to condense into liquid.

In winter, temperatures outside the home are below the dewpoint of the air inside. Unless there is a vapor barrier (at points A and B in the drawing), the moisture will migrate through the drywall or plaster, across the insulation and through the siding. For example, if the temperature outside is 25 °F, and the inside air temperature is 70 °F, at 29% humidity, a surface within the wall will be at or below the dewpoint (36 °F). Moisture will condense—usually on the sheathing—causing it and the siding to become saturated. Moisture cannot pass through a vapor barrier.

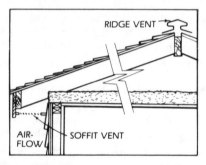

FOR GOOD AIRFLOW from the attic, a combination of vents, such as the soffit and ridge vents shown, is recommended.

DEW POINT CHART
(Outside Temperature at 25° F)

Room Temperature	Room Relative Humidity (%)	Dew Point Temperature (°F)
70° F	79	63
	68	59
	57	54
	48	49
	38	43
	29	**36**
	19	26
	9	11
75° F	79	68
	68	64
	57	60
	48	55
	38	47
	29	**40**
	19	30
	9	15

Attic airflow and mildew

Filling in roof deck spaces can alter the ventilation pattern of a house. The attic no longer breathes as easily as it did before the deck spaces were filled. This causes a moisture buildup, which results in mildew.

Gable vents are helpful, but only if they are adequately sized. The effective opening for louvers is not the same as the actual opening cut out for those louvers.

The gross area of the actual opening can be reduced by as much as 65 percent because of the resistance introduced by the louvers. If you have a gable vent with outside dimensions of 2 x 2 ft., depending on the type of louvers and insect screen used, you may only have an equivalent opening of about 1 x 1 ft.

An attic should have effective openings, equivalent to 1/300 of the attic floor area. A single vent opening in an attic, even though it satisfied the total area requirement, is not considered adequate. The best method for ventilating an attic is to use a combination of vents, such as soffit (fascia) and gable vents, or soffit vents and a ridge vent.

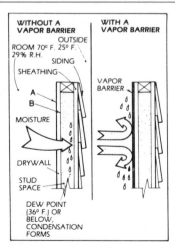

Water in your basement—how to stop it

■ ANYONE who has pumped out and mopped up a basement flood knows the hopeless feeling it generates and the damage water leaves in its wake. Out-of-season clothes, shoes, books, dry firewood, golf clubs, oil-pump motors—all suffer from a forced bath.

Listed below are 11 common situations which potentially lead to a wet basement. Find those cases which resemble your own and read what you can do about them.

1. Seepage from basement window wells occurs when rainwater collects in the wells and enters through cracks around the window or through the foundation itself.

Cures: Build up the curb around a window-well perimeter with masonry or corrugated metal. Where no drain exists, install one attached to piping leading away from the foundation.

2. Poor grading around the foundation accounts for most basement water problems. Faulty grading is described as any soil condition that dumps water against a foundation wall. The water eventually builds enough pressure—called hydrostatic pres-

THERE ARE many causes of a wet basement; 11 of the most common are: (1) basement window wells with clogged drain or no drain at all; (2) improper grading; (3) clogged drain—or none at all—in outside basement stairwell; (4) below-grade foundation cracks or missing mortar; (5) high water table or underground spring; (6) root-clogged drain tile; (7) downspout disconnected from gutter; (8) garden bed at foundation wall; (9) clogged dry well or no splash block at downspout; (10) infrequently cleaned gutter; (11) missing gutters, downspouts.

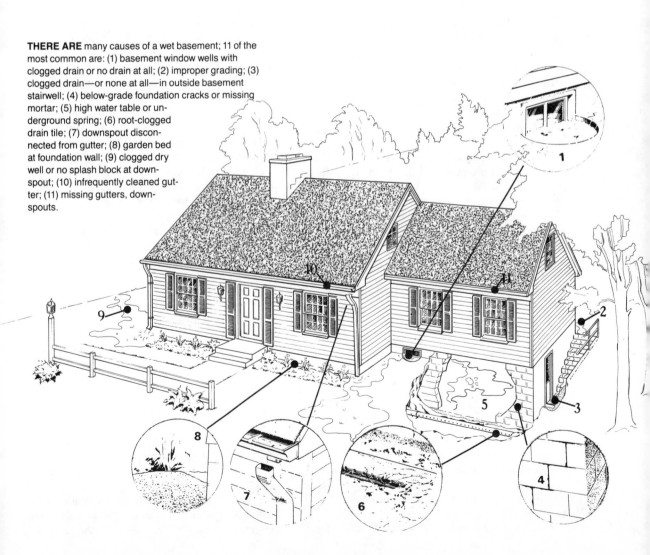

sure—so that no matter how well foundation walls are protected against seepage, it will find a way in.

The commonest form of poor grading is ground leading away from the house on the level, or worse, inclined uphill. These situations are not too hard to correct. The toughest problem occurs when a builder fails to provide ground-water drainage for a house built into a hillside or he digs a swale (depression) at the base of the hill, but underestimates the amount and force of water coursing down the hill toward the house.

Cures: Raise the grade around the foundation so that a fall of at least ½ in. to the foot continues down and away from the house at least 6 ft., and preferably 10. With fresh mortar, parge bare masonry around the foundation before packing new soil against it, or adhere a layer of 6-mil black polyethylene to the masonry surface. Over the new soil, plant a thirsty ground cover, such as pachysandra, vinca minor or periwinkle—or put down sod.

For the hillside house at the foot of a virtual waterfall during a rainstorm, the cure takes more time and energy. Redirect water around the house and downhill by a French drain—a ditch filled with crushed stone. This water-absorbing ditch parallels the line where hill and level lot meet.

Viewed from a helicopter, the drain looks like a U around the house, its base on the uphill side. Depth and width of the ditch will vary. Cover the stone-filled trench with straw, topsoil and sod. At the line below the hill, sod cover should be at the center of a slight swale, so hill-draining water has a chance to soak into the French drain.

As added insurance to catch a large volume of water, lay drain pipe over 2 in. of stone at the base of the ditch before backfilling with the remaining stone.

At lower ends of the drain lines, divert outfalling water with rock so the current doesn't carve furrows in the lawn. Or, connect the drains to solid piping that carries water underground to drainage.

3. Exterior basement entries are often water routes to basements. You may have too low a curb around your stairwell opening, a clogged drain, or may lack a drain in the stairwell. Double metal cellar doors that have been climbed upon or banged with a heavy object may have damaged runoff channels that direct water into the basement.

Cures: Same as for No. 1. Use caulking to seal around metal cellar doors. Bend deformed channels back in position if possible.

4. Cracks in masonry or at masonry joints are a common cause of water infiltration. Masonry that is porous and subjected to ground-water pressure is also a sure candidate.

Cures: If you have eliminated water against the

foundation wall as much as possible and still have moisture or seepage, consider applying an interior masonry sealer. A comparison of three types appears in the chart. Follow manufacturer's directions for wall preparations to the letter.

5. A high water table or an underground spring are the rarest sources of basement floods, and are most difficult to stop. If water in your basement is essentially clear, it probably flows from one of these sources.

Cures: The pressure-relief system described should handle the problem.

6. Clogged drain tile around the foundation footing forces ground water against the foundation or beneath the footing into the space below the floor slab. Old clay drain tile laid in sections is usually to blame. Silt and soil build up between sections that have worked apart. A tree root may have broken through a tile (and could do the same to newer plastic drain piping).

Diagnosing this problem is difficult; the only sure way is to dig down, unearth the tile and examine it. That's time-consuming, and should you have it done, expensive. A simple test, however, tells you the direction from which water comes. If water lying on the basement floor is muddy or laced with silt, it's a 99-to-1 bet it came from the ground around the foundation, and just possibly seeped into the basement because of blocked drain tile. Clear water usually indicates a spring or high water table.

Cure: Double check water sources through 3. If you can divert ground water from the drain tile, whether the tile is blocked or not becoms irrelevant.

Having completed your checking and correcting only to discover during the next downpour that the basement still leaks, proceed to the next least-expensive step: Seal the basement walls, the periphery of the floor.

In the unlikely event your basement still leaks, review your latest work. Have you missed anything? Skimped on application? If not, you need the pressure-relief system.

7. Broken or rusted-out downspouts and gutters that fail to carry off water are obvious trouble sources.

Cure: By all means, repair breaks and replace rusted-out sections of the rain-carrying system. Often, the weak point is the right-angle gutter beneath a roof valley. During a hard rain, valleys can catch and send more water coursing than a gutter will carry. If possible, cut a downspout into the system at the angle, and divert the outflow.

8. Flower beds parallel to the foundation are a form of poor grading that can also lead to water where you don't want it. Gardens crested in the center are the worst offenders—they invite water to pool and seep along the foundation wall.

Cure: Get rid of the garden. Build up the grade as noted in No. 2, and plant ground cover or lay down sod.

9. A downspout that pours water only a few inches from the foundation wall is little help. It may cause the soil to become saturated (boggy) with water, thereby increasing the likelihood of basement seepage. A stopped-up or flooded dry well close to the house produces the same effect.

Cures: At least, put a stone or concrete splash block under the downspout. Better, attach a rolled vinyl hose to the downspout end. Force of the flow unrolls the hose and deposits water some distance away from the foundation.

Best of all, connect the downspout with solid piping leading to an area drain, or a dry well excavated at least 25 ft. from the foundation. (A dry well is 6 to 8 ft. deep, 4 to 6 ft. in diameter, and walled with unmortared stone or concrete clock. The top is closed with a stone slab or cast concrete lid. Then covered with a layer of topsoil and sod to match the lawn.)

10. Clogged gutters resemble Nos. 7, 8 and 9 in their damaging effect. They are, however, a lot easier to remedy.

Cure: Climb to the roof and, using a garden trowel or gloved hand, scoop gutter-muck into a bucket or to the ground. Install "bird-cages" or screening at top openings of all your downspouts to prevent the possibility of clogging with twigs and leaves.

11. The lack of gutters and leaders can cause ground beneath the eaves to erode. During a rain, the depressions fill with water that eventually will find its way inside your basement.

Cure: Install a rain-carrying system.

BASEMENT WALL AND FLOOR SEALERS

Material	Before Applying, Fill Holes and Cracks With	Apply Over Paint?	Apply Over Wet Wall?	Coverage	Masonry Penetration	Recommended Number of Coats	Warranty	Paint Over it?
Drylok (Portland cement plus additives, i.e. synthetic rubber)	Hydraulic cement	Only over a cement-base paint in good condition	No, but okay over damp wall	75 to 100 sq. ft. per gallon	Deeper than paint	2	Five years when applied correctly	Yes
Devcon (Two-component epoxy compound)	Hydraulic cement or Portland cement mortar	Only if paint condition is very good	No, but okay over damp wall	150 to 200 sq. ft. per gallon	Forms tough outer coating	2	None	Yes
Xypex (Portland cement, silica, organic chemicals)	Thicker mix of Xypex	No	Yes; will not work otherwise	6 sq. ft. per gallon	Several coats, thickness of foundation wall	2	Warranty by applicator who does job	Yes

HOW TO PUT an electronic "fence" around your home: Studies show that alarms triggered by a network of detectors throughout a house will scare away 98 percent of all burglars. While most homes will not have all the security devices indicated on the house plan above, it shows the wide variety of aids available. They are: 1. master control; 2. remote master; 3. indoor remote switch; 4. outdoor remote switch; 5. manual emergency (panic) button; 6. reset button; 7. shunt switch; 8. light-flasher relay; 9. surface-mount magnetic detector; 10. recessed magnetic detector; 11. glass-break sensor; 12. ultrasonic detector; 13. alarm-wired screen; 14. pressure-sensitive floormat; 15. outdoor alarm horn; 16. indoor horn; 17. automatic telephone dialer; 18. photocell detector.

Burglar-alarm systems for your home

■ "WE DON'T NEED a burglar alarm when we're home," said a Philadelphia contractor. Not true. While he and his family were eating dinner last summer, a "cat burglar" hoisted himself up to a small second-story balcony outside the master bedroom, entered quietly through French doors, swept valuable jewelry into a pillowcase and left as he came.

"The house is completely locked. We aren't worried about thefts," said a Minneapolis couple. Wrong again. Returning from a two-week vacation, they found their house stripped. The thief had broken a window, reached in to release the sash lock and entered easily.

"I always leave the door unlocked. Nothing ever happens here," said a bachelor in Laramie, Wyo. Back from an evening movie, he found his house ransacked.

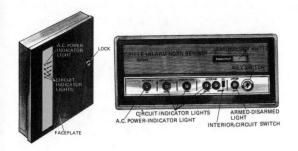

MASTER CONTROL PANEL (above left) connects all components in system. LEDs indicate if system is operating properly and, if not, where trouble lies. It has standby battery and connections for extra circuits. Remote master (above right) is similar, but styled for use in bedroom, kitchen, or other living areas. It has its own alarm horn behind decorative grille, panic button and indicator lights.

In all three cases, the owners slammed the barn door after the horse was stolen. They now have burglar-alarm systems.

A full alarm system runs one or more perimeter circuits from a central control, arming all windows and outside doors. It may also include one or more interior circuits, laying traps for an intruder who manages to elude the perimeter loops. A full system generally ties in fire protection as well.

A number of systems are sold in kit form, with instructions for do-it-yourself installation. Inexpensive systems are the easiest to install, mainly because they consist of fewer and simpler parts. As the price goes up, so does the sophistication and the time it will take to hook everything up. The actual wiring, however, is fairly simple, since alarm systems almost universally operate on 12 volts, permitting the use of easy-to-run, low-voltage cable. A transformer is connected between house current and the central control, and there's usually a standby battery to provide backup power in a blackout.

Here are the parts common to most systems:

Central control panel

The central control panel is the heart of any full alarm system. It contains a relay that transmits signals from the detectors to an audible alarm in the house or to the security station monitoring your system. Most controls also display signal lights, indicating power on/off and whether or not the circuits are armed.

Control panels are used for both wired and radio-transmitted alarms. Choose a wireless network if it's too much of a hassle to conceal the wires and surface wiring will appear too unsightly.

In a radio system, the central control plugs into a 115-volt outlet and has a 12-volt backup battery. Battery-operated radio transmitters, wired to perimeter detectors, send a signal to the control panel when a break-in occurs, and the panel sounds the alarm. This system goes in more easily than the wired type, but does have a drawback: Not everyone remembers to replace batteries regularly, and a dead one could knock out your protection.

REMOTE KEY switch fits standard electrical wall box, allows you to arm or disarm system at points distant from master control. Similar switch is made in weatherproof style for outdoor use so you can control the system from a porch deck or patio.

PANIC BUTTON lets you sound alarm manually if you suspect intruder is trying to break in. You can have one by your bed, others elsewhere. Similar control boxes house reset buttons for rearming system after it's been triggered and shunt switches to temporarily disarm door or window.

In a wired system, the central control panel is connected through a transformer to your house wiring and contains a rechargeable battery for emergency backup power. Wires connect it to your door and window detectors, forming a continuous loop of protection. A break in the circuit at any point in the loop causes the alarm to sound.

Remote controls

A master remote panel is similar to the central control panel, but can be installed in any remote location where you want to keep tabs on the system. Often it's attractively styled so it can be openly displayed in living areas, such as the kitchen or master bedroom. Its signals tell you the same information as the main control panel—sometimes more. It can also house an

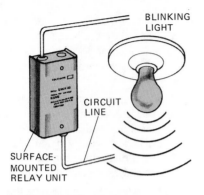

LIGHT-FLASHER relay turns on house lights (up to 1000 watts) if a detector is tripped. It can also blink lights on and off to scare away a thief.

alarm of its own, usually behind a decorative grille. What the panel gives you is a second opportunity to oversee the system.

Exit/entry devices

Obviously, you and the members of your family must have a way to enter and leave the house without triggering the alarm yourselves. Several options are open to you: digital signals code-set to allow you time to enter or leave, key locks that let you disarm the system momentarily, or a simple button switch to deactivate the system for a

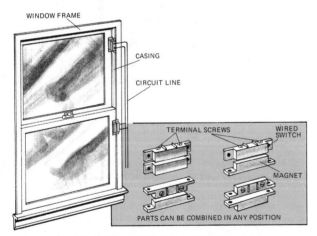

MAGNETIC DETECTORS install on windows and doors to form continuous loop of protection to encircle the house. Magnets and their magnetically controlled switches are arranged in closely spaced pairs. The surface mount type shown here is the easiest to install.

preset interval, usually just long enough to let you get in or out the door.

Whatever its form, the exit/entry device is both a necessity—and a nuisance. It's been labeled by many alarm-system owners as the "false-alarm trigger." The device—or actually

the failure to use it properly—seems to set off more "cry wolf" calls than any other single component. You go to let the dog out, forget to disarm the system and suddenly—wham!—off goes the alarm with a deafening blast, disturbing neighbors and sometimes bringing the police on the run.

A shunt switch allows you to open a door briefly without tripping the alarm. This is a form

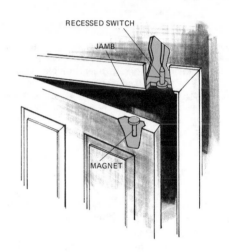

MAGNETIC DETECTORS can also be installed in door and window jambs as shown here. They look neater and are harder for a burglar to spot than surface types, but are more difficult to install.

of disarming control, but it deactivates only one detector, not the whole system. The switch releases the door detector from the perimeter circuit loop until the switch is flipped on again. The same switch lets you open a bedroom window at night for fresh air without setting off the alarm or having to deactivate the entire system. You must remember to reset a shunt switch, however. Unlike a timed exit/entry control, it will not reset itself automatically.

Emergency switches

Emergency switches—more familiarly known as panic buttons—do just what their name implies. They allow you to trigger the alarm manually any time you think an intruder is attempting to break in or in other emergencies where a loud alarm might be useful in calling for help. Install the buttons at key locations, such as next to your bed and in an upstairs hallway.

Another type of remote control is a reset button that puts the system back into operation after the alarm has been set off by an intruder—or a forgetful child. In some systems, this is a key-operated switch instead of a button, but it does the same thing. Install a reset next to the central control panel if it doesn't contain its own reset (some do). Another possibility: alongside entry doors, where many false alarms are triggered.

Magnetic detectors

Magnetic detectors are used to protect entry doors, sliding glass doors, garage doors and any form of window that opens. These consist of two parts: an unwired magnet and a wired switch that is controlled by the magnet. The two are arranged with a slight gap between them so as to maintain a constant magnetic field.

The clever part about this system is that it's constantly energized so that a break anywhere in the circuit—not just at a detector—will automatically trigger the alarm. Thus, if a thief attempts to deactivate the alarm by cutting the wires, it instantly sets it off.

GLASS-BREAK DETECTOR

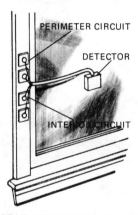

GLASS-BREAK detector is tiny device that sticks to large picture window or sliding glass door. Sensitive to vibration, it sounds alarm if glass is broken, but won't trip if jarred only by wind gusts.

Hidden detectors

If you prefer a concealed system, recessed types of magnetic detectors are also available. These fit flush into the edges of doors and windows and are almost invisible. They take a lot more work to install, but they improve the looks and, more important, disguise your protection from an intruder peering inside. If thieves can see the magnets, they might attempt to defeat the system.

Another type of door and window detector is mechanical and less reliable. Called a plunger detector, it signals for an alarm when its plunger is depressed as little as ⅛ inch. Its problem is that

moisture in the air can corrode the plunger, eventually jamming it.

There's more. You've seen how commercial establishments are protected with strips of metallic foil around the edges of windows. This system is also available for home installation and is not a bad idea for a large expanse of fixed glass. Smashing the glass breaks the foil tape, instantly sounding the alarm. The tape can be wired into the same system as magnetic detectors so you can have magnets on windows that move and the foil on those that don't.

Sophisticated sensors

Area protection inside the house is provided by some of the more dramatic devices. Newest among these is the infrared heat sensor. It sends out finger-slim beams of invisible infrared light, ready in an instant to detect any change in temperature. It won't trip when morning sun streams in a window, but will sound the minute a human body at 98° F. passes through the beams.

Another type, the ultrasonic detector, sends out sound waves inaudible to human ears. The device is both a transmitter and receiver. When the pattern of sound waves received is different

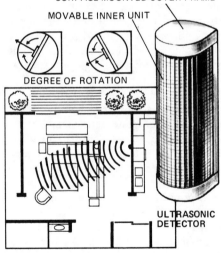

ULTRASONIC DETECTOR protects broad interior spaces. It sends inaudible sound waves through a room. If waves are disturbed by someone crossing their path, it sounds an alarm. Transmitter swivels to aim it for desired area of coverage. Other area-type detectors use microwaves or heat-sensing infrared.

from that of the waves sent out, it indicates that the waves have been disturbed by someone crossing their path, and the alarm sounds.

A third device, the microwave detector, is also a transceiver. It floods the area with high-frequency radio waves (not injurious to health). The

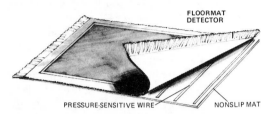

PRESSURE-SENSITIVE floormat hidden under a rug or stair runner flashes the alarm if stepped on. They're good for doorways, halls and other high-traffic areas.

detector, monitoring the reflected energy, notes when the waves have been distorted by someone moving through them and sounds the alarm. A problem: Pets or small children can trigger the alarm.

Sliding glass doors and other doorways can also be protected by photoelectric cells using beams of invisible infrared light. A transmitter and reflector are installed on opposite sides of the door. If someone breaks the reflected beam, the alarm sounds.

Pressure-sensitive mats

Pressure-sensitive floormats, laid under rugs or stair carpet, will signal the central control when a person (even a dog) walks on them. These are good for doorways, halls and sliding glass doors, but can be a problem when someone sleepily goes downstairs for a late-night snack and forgets to disarm them.

An audio detector should be mentioned, too. Stationed centrally in the house, it detects the sound frequency made by breaking glass. It's a good idea if your house has a lot of vulnerable glass area, but shouldn't be needed if the perimeter is well protected by other devices.

Alarm-wired door and window screens offer added protection. You might want to consider them if your house is hidden from street view or in a remote location where a burglar would have more time to work unnoticed. An alarm sounds if the screen is cut or removed.

Indoor and outdoor alarms

The alarm itself is either a loud bell or blaring horn. You can choose an indoor type, an outdoor type—or both. An indoor alarm is loud enough to wake you when you're home and is usually frightening enough to scare off an intruder even when you're away. However, it probably won't be heard by neighbors.

An outdoor alarm will rouse the entire neighborhood and perhaps even get the attention of a nearby patrol car. On the other hand, you can't always count on neighbors to call the police for you—they may not be home or, more likely, may tire of the game after about the third false alarm. For this reason, most installations include both an inside and outside alarm. An added bonus: If a thief cuts the wires to an outside alarm, the inside one will still sound.

What happens if a thief cuts your 115-volt house wiring? Will the alarm be deactivated? No. It will immediately switch over to power from the 12-volt backup battery and remain armed. If the intruder then interrupts the perimeter wiring at any point, the alarm will go off. This gives you protection if the power goes out for any reason, and at the same time prevents the alarm from sounding during a storm-related blackout.

Telephone alerts

Three less noisy options are also open to you. One is a simple light-circuit relay. When signaled, it switches on all house lights connected to its circuit. It can also be set to flash the lights on and off. Often, this is enough to frighten off an intruder.

OUTDOOR ALARM horn sounds electronic wail at 102 decibels, loud enough to rouse entire neighborhood. Indoor horn at 85 db. wakes sleepers. Most installations include both. If outdoor alarm is cut, indoor one will sound.

The second is an automatic telephone dialer combined with a tape recorder. You prerecord a message on tape, saying your house is being burglarized. When an actual break-in occurs, the dialer silently rings a preselected number—a friend, neighbor or the police. Unfortunately, the police in some areas may not permit automatic dialers to be set to their number (because of the nuisance of false alarms).

Better is a silent, digital telephone dialer that sends a coded signal to a central security station. This is the most expensive route to take, but also the closest to being foolproof. False alarms are intercepted before neighbors or the police are unnecessarily alerted.

Burglar protection in your home

■ BURGLARS LOOK FOR what police call "targets of opportunity"—easy pickings. They're not out for hard work, or they'd be working. And despite their line of work, they're cowards, avoiding risk as much as they can. So the more trouble you can give burglars, and the more obvious that trouble is, the more likely they are to go somewhere else.

Sending the burglar somewhere else isn't too hard, either. Locks, alarms and common sense are all you need—and all but the common sense are widely available and easy to install.

Burglars hate noise, light or anything else that can call attention to them. So an alarm can scare off burglars when they've just started work—and knowing there's an alarm can do it even before they've started. If they're still not scared off, the alarm can summon help to stop them.

Yet even alarms, the most sophisticated defense in your home security arsenal, are easy to buy and install yourself—and comparatively inexpensive, too.

There are three basic types of alarms: self-contained units that protect a single door or window, motion-sensing types that cover a single room or area, and perimeter types that can cover every critical point about your home.

The single-entry, self-contained type is a small

THREE WAYS TO PROTECT YOUR HOME ELECTRONICALLY

COMBINATION SELF-CONTAINED alarm and patio latch protects entrance that's often neglected by homeowners. Self-contained alarms are the cheapest type, not necessarily the best.

MOTION-DETECTOR triggers alarm if its wave field should be disturbed by a moving burglar—or a pet. This is easiest type alarm to install; most cover a room at a time; intruder usually must be in house before it will go off.

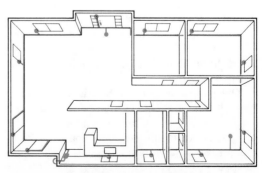

PERIMETER ALARMS give burglary warnings at as many parts or openings of the house as you like, can warn of other problems, too. "Wireless" types install easily.

box containing a battery, horn or siren, and some kind of triggering device; you fit one to each door or window that you want to protect. Some, in fact, are combined with door or window locks—a bargain only if *both* the lock and alarm are top quality.

Self-contained entry alarms are the least expensive alarms you can buy, and are easy to install: Alarm/lock combinations usually install in the same hole a normal rim-lock's cylinder would use, and door alarms usually require no keyhole (a delay lets you get in and turn them off).

Small alarms may not do

But these small alarms aren't very loud—enough to warn anyone at home and possibly in the next apartment, but not enough to carry down a noisy block. And with everything right where the burglar is, they're vulnerable to any thief who can keep cool enough to silence them. (Obviously, solid construction is a must.) Cheap as they are, their cost mounts rapidly as the number of doors and windows covered increases; in a big house, it could quickly approach the cost of more sophisticated systems—and you'd still have to check and set each alarm individually every time you left the house.

Motion-sensing alarms can be even easier to install: Just set a self-contained motion-sensor in an inconspicuous corner of the room you want to protect, turn it on, and leave the room in the few seconds before the alarm sets itself. After that, any motion within the alarm's area first turns on a light (to frighten a thief, and to remind you to shut it off when you come in), then squawks its head off seconds later. Motion-sensors vary in price; some are self-contained with built-in horns or sirens, others triggering remote indoor or outdoor warnings, with satellites monitoring other rooms.

Motion-sensor alarms fill the room with a pattern of waves (usually ultrasonic, in home models), and sense the frequency shifts when the waves are reflected back by moving objects (just as car horns shift pitch when traveling toward or away from you).

Older ultrasonics could be triggered by flapping drapes; more modern units are immune to this, but will be set off by pets within their coverage areas—or family members going for a midnight snack. The ultrasonic signals could annoy dogs, too.

Motion-sensors are called "intrusion alarms" because they don't go off till someone's intruded.

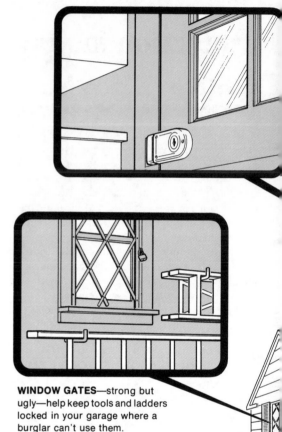

DOUBLE-CYLINDER locks can't be opened by a bu breaking through the glass panes of a door.

WINDOW GATES—strong but ugly—help keep tools and ladders locked in your garage where a burglar can't use them.

LIGHTS AT DOORS help you identify after-dark call and expose night burglars working on your locks

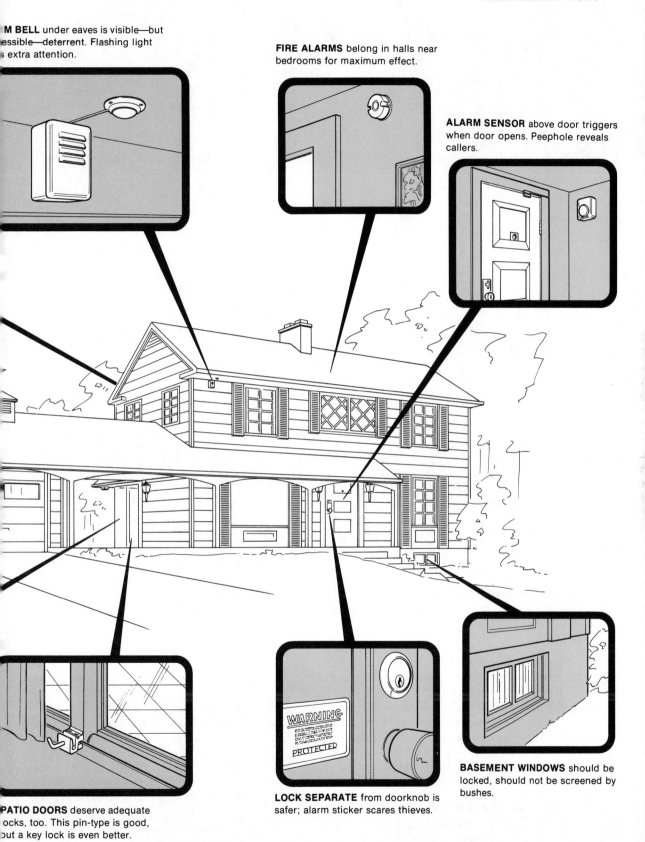

M BELL under eaves is visible—but
essible—deterrent. Flashing light
extra attention.

FIRE ALARMS belong in halls near
bedrooms for maximum effect.

ALARM SENSOR above door triggers
when door opens. Peephole reveals
callers.

WARNING

PROTECTED

PATIO DOORS deserve adequate
ocks, too. This pin-type is good,
ut a key lock is even better.

LOCK SEPARATE from doorknob is
safer; alarm sticker scares thieves.

BASEMENT WINDOWS should be
locked, should not be screened by
bushes.

ALARMS—A SOPHISTICATED DEFENSE

MAGNETIC SENSOR triggers when a window is opened. Extra magnet lets you open it a few inches for ventilation.

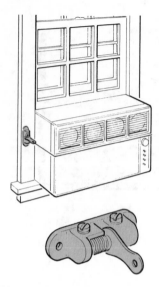

TRAP SWITCH—here guarding an airconditioning unit—triggers when the string pulls the tab out.

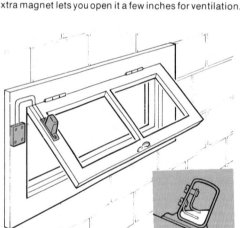

MERCURY SWITCH installed on basement top-hinged window sounds an alarm when the window is opened so that the liquid wets both switch contacts at once.

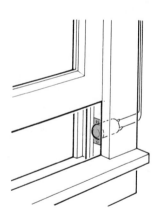

BULLET SWITCH hidden in door or window frame has tapered plunger that sets off alarm as the door or the window is opened. The wiring is invisible.

Perimeter and door alarms go off as soon as the openings they protect are breached. Not that intrusion alarms aren't useful—they're just not the first recommendation for home use.

But they are excellent if one room requires special protection (because of valuables stored there), and for relatively untrafficked rooms, such as outbuildings or garages. There are 12-volt models for use in boats or campers.

Perimeter alarm recommended

Pros usually recommend the perimeter alarm. Perimeter systems have a central control box triggered by a network of alarm sensors throughout a house and, in turn, setting off bells or other warnings where needed. (Some systems, though, combine control and bell in one box.)

Perimeter systems do the most complete overall job—they can cover every door and window, check for intruders inside the house, warn you of fire, even call the police if no one's home. They can also warn if your freezer's melting or your pipes are freezing, and if anyone falls into your pool.

Their versatility—and the fact that they're usually hooked to a good, loud, remote bell or

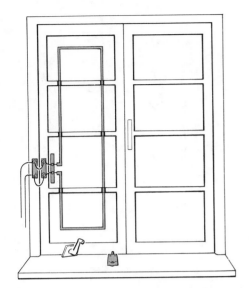

FOIL TAPE breaks if the window's broken, setting off an alarm. Plunger of tamper switch on the sill releases if the window is opened.

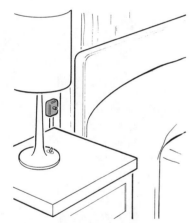

PANIC BUTTON can trip alarm from bed or front door. Some alarms have separate, always-on panic circuits.

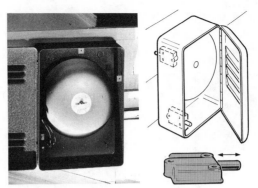

ALARM BELL or siren should be mounted where it's conspicuous, easy to hear, but inaccessible to burglars. Tamper switch in the box triggers the alarm if box lid is opened or the box is pried from the wall.

SEVERAL OUTFITS are sold for do-it-yourself installation. System shown gives separate fire and burglary warnings.

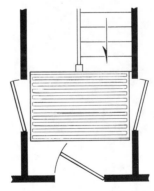

PRESSURE-SENSITIVE mat switch should go where burglars are almost sure to tread on them, as in this entrance hall.

FIRE WARNINGS

FIRE DETECTORS come in several types, for connection to perimeter systems as well as for self-contained use. This is a self-contained ionization detector type shown in the chart at right as being highly effective.

DETECTORS AND THE FOUR STAGES OF FIRE
DETECTORS AND THE FOUR STAGES OF FIRE

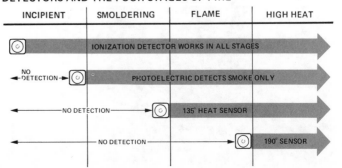

INCIPIENT	SMOLDERING	FLAME	HIGH HEAT
IONIZATION DETECTOR WORKS IN ALL STAGES			
NO DETECTION	PHOTOELECTRIC DETECTS SMOKE ONLY		
NO DETECTION		135° HEAT SENSOR	
NO DETECTION			190° SENSOR

DOOR LOCKS WITH VARYING DEGREES OF SECURITY

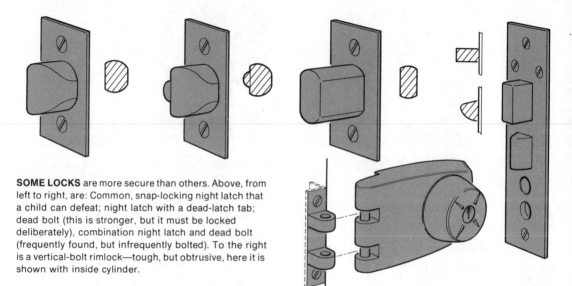

SOME LOCKS are more secure than others. Above, from left to right, are: Common, snap-locking night latch that a child can defeat; night latch with a dead-latch tab; dead bolt (this is stronger, but it must be locked deliberately), combination night latch and dead bolt (frequently found, but infrequently bolted). To the right is a vertical-bolt rimlock—tough, but obtrusive, here it is shown with inside cylinder.

"POLICE LOCKS" are tough, but ugly to look at: rack-and-pinion bolt type (directly below); diagonal bolt types, which transfer stress to the floor (bottom and below right).

EASY-TO-FIND SECURITY AIDS

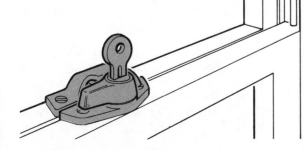

ENGRAVING NAMES or identifying numbers on any valuables such as cameras, tools and the like can help recover them and at the same time convict the thieves.

CHAIN LOCKS should be installed on a slant; allow only 2 or 3-in. opening. Peephole is best for identification, since chain lock can be broken.

PEEPHOLES LET YOU see who's out there without opening your door. The best types are those with widest view angle (to 180°).

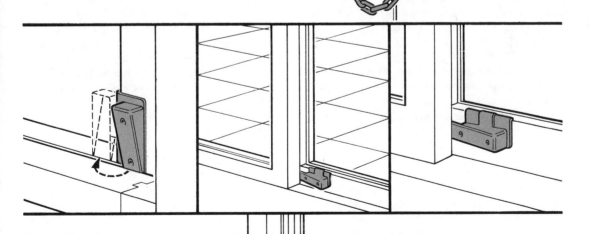

WEDGE LOCK for windows and sliding doors (above) is inexpensive, easy to install, but vulnerable if burglar breaks glass. Key locks (like that shown at left as replacement for the common, swivel type of window lock) are a lot more secure and cost little. Keep keys handy in case of a fire or other emergency.

siren—make perimeter systems more effective. But it's even more significant that they make it easier for you to use them more effectively.

That's because they're centrally controlled. You're more likely to set one alarm when you leave the house than to check and set one for every opening. And most perimeter systems are "supervised": They tell you if you've left a door or window open (though not whether you left it closed but unlocked). You're also more likely to check and replace one battery than several, and the better systems use a battery only for a back-up, otherwise running on a.c.

Most such systems are "hard-wired," with direct connections from sensors (which come in a wide variety) to the central control. But there are also "carrier" systems, whose sensors send signals to the control panel through your home's a.c. wiring, and RF wireless types, which send brief radio signals to the control box when breached.

Pros and cons of RF and carriers

Both RF and carrier systems are easier to install than hard-wired types. But carrier systems won't work if your a.c. current goes off; and RF types, which cost more, aren't "supervised," because their sensors signal only when a door or window opens—so they can't tell you one's already open when you turn them on. However, RF systems can be set to go off in a nearby neighbor's house, if you're away. (So can "carrier" types, if you and your neighbor get power through the same transformer.)

Wired alarms also come in two types: open and closed circuit. Open-circuit systems, a trifle cheaper, trigger when their sensor switches close, completing the alarm circuit. Closed-circuit types trigger when a sensor switch opens—or when there's a break in the wires. That gives them an extra degree of self-checking, and insures against a burglar defeating them by clipping wires. (He can defeat a closed-circuit system with a jumper—but only if he knows it's a closed-circuit type, and if it's accessible.)

The more doors and windows your system covers, the better you're protected—but the more your system will cost. Install it yourself, and the additional cost is minor.

So which openings should you protect? Your doors, of course, every ground-floor window, and every window within reach of (not just directly over) porches, garage and shed roofs, fire escapes—even trees.

It's up to you whether to protect all your second-story windows; some burglars do use ladders, either by bringing their own or taking them from nearby sheds or garages.

On a limited budget, that extra money might be better spent on an alarm system with more features: a rechargeable back-up battery with trickle-charger, for instance, or circuits (required by some local noise pollution laws) that shut the alarm off after about 15 minutes.

Fire alarms can be part of any perimeter alarm system, simply by adding sensors that detect heat, fast temperature increases or smoke. But to avoid confusion, systems that sound separate warnings for fire and intrusion are better—and self-contained fire alarms, which don't go dead if the fire takes your power out, are better still. For fire, the emphasis should be on *inside* sirens, to wake you and your family and get you out.

Once your door is set to trigger the alarm, how do you get back in the house? Some alarms have outside keylocks that disconnect the door's alarm so you can enter. Others have a delayed action; you can shut them off as soon as you come in (burglars, presumably, won't know where to find the switch before the delay time's up).

Delay systems require less wiring, and can't be picked from outside. But key switches do show the burglar that your alarm is real, not just a decal stuck on as a bluff. (Even the decals will make some burglars think twice before they try to break in.)

A light at the door to show the alarm's on can tell late-coming family members whether someone's come home and shut the system off. If you all come home together, it can tip you off that a burglar—who might still be inside—has come in and shut it off before you. (But if you're likely to forget to turn the alarm on, the light can tip off the burglar.)

Flashing lights added to your alarm's bell or siren can speed response, showing at a glance just which house the noise is coming from. Telephone dialers are another good (but expensive for professional-quality) supplement, dialing neighbors, friends or police with a recorded trouble message when the main alarm goes off. Most good ones have two tracks—one for burglary, one for fire. Dialers are especially worthwhile for summer or isolated homes.

Check your local laws before setting up a dialer. False alarms are common in home alarm systems because people come in on irregular schedules. So many towns prohibit programming dialers from calling the police or fire department directly.

DO-IT-YOURSELF 'LOCKS' ARE EASY TO MAKE, INEXPENSIVE

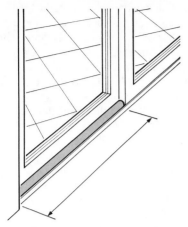

BROOMSTICK OR metal rod in patio door tracks keeps door from opening, even if lock is picked or broken.

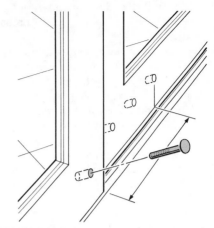

CARRIAGE BOLT or large nail in slanted holes locks patio doors. Extra holes allow up to 6-inch air opening.

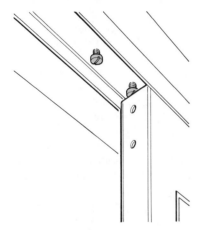

SCREWS IN PATIO door's upper track keep thieves from lifting door off; a good trick for sliding windows, too.

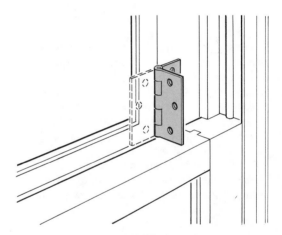

DOOR HINGE makes a good folding lock to hold sash window tightly shut. Improvisation costs just pennies.

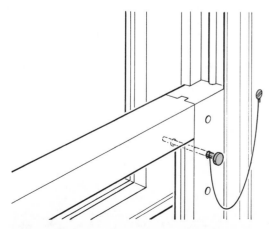

NAIL OR BOLT "latch" trick works well for windows, too; but here you allow only 2 to 3 inches for air.

Even better than setting off an alarm when a burglars break in, though, is keeping them out altogether. Sometimes it's less expensive, too. All it takes are good locks and remembering to use them.

Check locks after moving

The best time to look at your locks is right after you move; you never know who might have gotten keys from the old tenant or, if it's a new home, from the builder.

You don't have to replace the locks. Just take the cylinders to a locksmith for rekeying, or replace the cylinders with new ones. You can get pick-resistant cylinders (*no* key lock is pick-*proof*) for a little more than regular ones. But comparatively few burglars pick locks. The pick man is highly skilled and expects a return for his skill. Unless you've got a lot to steal, he probably won't bother you.

Combination locks are pickproof, but expensive, and fumbling with one can cost you precious time if you're trying to get in quickly to avoid a mugger or the rain.

But before rekeying your lock, consider whether the lock itself might not need replacement or protection. A simple "night-latch" type that locks whenever it springs shut should definitely be replaced. Slipping a plastic credit card between the door and the frame can open it.

"Dead-latching" snap-locks are a slight improvement—a small tab keeps the spring latch from pushing back when the door's closed. Square-ended dead bolts that slide straight into the jamb are more secure, and the longer the bolt, the better it will hold against a burglar trying to burst or pry his way in.

Vertical dead bolts are even more secure, since they can't be pried open. They can be pried off, though, so be sure you've fastened yours with the longest, biggest screws that will fit. If possible, the strike plate that meshes with the lock should be the type that wraps around two sides of the doorframe. One model has a cylinder shield that bolts to the lock for added protection.

Vertical-bolt locks are "rim" types that fasten to the inside of the door and frame; this makes them easy to install, but less attractive than locks that fit within the door.

Be sure door is strong

But the strongest, safest locks won't hold weak doors securely. Hollow-core, wood-veneer flush doors and cheap paneled doors are a breeze to break through; hardboard-faced flush doors and better paneled ones are stronger, but solid or metal-faced doors are safer still. Make sure the door fits snugly in the frame and that the lock's bolt protrudes as far as possible into the frame.

If your door has glass panes in or near it, consider double-cylinder locks, which are opened with a key from inside, too, so a thief can't break the glass, reach in and open the lock. And where a burglar is most likely to come in a window or through a smashed-in door panel, use of double cylinder locks will limit his haul to what he can take *out* that way, too.

But to be sure of safe escape in case of fire, you should leave your keys in the lock's inside cylinder whenever you're home—and don't use double cylinders if you have children or elderly relatives in the house. For fire safety, it's best, then, to install "panic-proof" locks that open if you twist the inside knob either way—a feature on better locks.

And there is another way to protect glazed doors: substitute impact-resistant polycarbonate for the glass, or cover the glass with polycarbonate held by extra moldings.

To protect your lock from outside attack, use one whose cylinder is in the door itself, not in the knob (which can be pried off), and cover it with a cylinder guard, bolted through the door.

Back doors and hidden entrances need even more protection than front doors, since concealment gives burglars more time to work on them.

But windows deserve protection, too. Standard, swiveling window latches can be opened from outside or through a broken or cut pane—key locks can't (and polycarbonate panes add extra protection). But if you lock your windows, leave the keys nearby and make sure everyone knows where to find them in case of fire—it's better to be burgled than to burn.

Commercial hardware isn't your only choice, either. Some standard do-it-yourself tricks are illustrated above; you may be able to come up with others.

But whatever locks, alarms or other tricks you may have up your sleeve, you must be sure to *use them*. Burglars very often slip in through unlocked doors and past unset alarms.

Burglarproof your house the low-cost ways

■ IT MAKES NO SENSE to spend a couple hundred dollars to install the latest in key cylinder technology in your door locks when all a burglar has to do is kick in an airconditioner and climb in through your side window. Little things, like the security tricks that follow, can often make the difference between a successful break-in and a foiled attempt. Although they won't make your house absolutely burglarproof, they will beef up your protection. The tighter your security, the more likely an intruder is to be deterred. As unneighborly as it sounds, most of us would much prefer to have a thief turn away from our own home to look for easier pickings down the street.

The simple steps shown here can be taken right now to eliminate, or at least strengthen, weak links in the perimeter defense of your home. Many will cost you almost nothing and most of the required materials for these projects can be found in the typical home workshop.

The projects fall into three basic categories: simple locking devices, lock reinforcement and improvement, and acrylic plastic shields. We've also included a rudimentary alarm that may make a thief think twice before ripping you off. Many of the principles involved can be modified to meet the requirements of your situation. The hints may also give rise to solutions that you can develop on your own.

One caution to keep in mind: Never install a device that will in any way hamper your exit during a fire or other emergency.

NO MATTER how good the lock, it's only as strong as the grip of the screws holding it in place. Most doors and jambs are constructed of softwood, which has poor screw-holding ability. To provide a better anchor for screws, counterbore the screw holes and insert hardwood dowels. Use ⅜-in.-dia. spiral-grooved dowels and resorcinol glue. Note that the door shown in the photo has a plywood veneer, but the interior consists of soft ponderosa pine. This is typical of many doors—and one reason a large number of homeowners have decided to replace wooden doors and jambs with steel units.

GARAGE DOOR LOCKS are easy to pick because builders usually use the cheapest-quality locks money can buy. It does a thief no good to pick your garage door lock, however, if you prevent him from raising your overhead door with this foolproof method: Drill a hole in the track slightly above one of the rollers and inset a ¼-in.-dia. steel rod to act as a stop. For a double door, drill the hole in both tracks and use a longer rod. A slight downward bend at each end will keep the rod in place.

Caution: Do not use this method with automatic-lifting doors; it can damage the lifting mechanism.

ONE OF THE easiest entries for a burglar is to push back a spring-latch lock when the doorjamb is the nonrabbeted type. To do it he slips a thin piece of plastic such as a credit card beneath stop and past door edge (arrow). To prevent such entries, drive four or five 6d finishing nails through the stop in front of the strike plate hole. Now a card can't be slid under stop. Use pilot holes to avoid splitting the stop and set nailheads below surface and fill with plastic wood filler to conceal nails. If greater strength is desired, substitute 1¼ in. No. 8 fh screws for the nails and insert them in counterbored holes.

 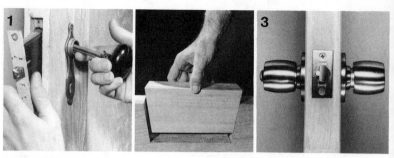

THIS SUPPLEMENTARY, heavy-duty strike is sized to fit under the standard strike for a key-in-knob lock. The off-center holes permit the use of heavy, 3-in.-long screws which penetrate well into the stud behind the jamb. A second pair of holes (partly obscured) allows the original strike to be reinstalled with the original screws. Deepen the mortise with a chisel to accommodate the extra thickness.

OLD FASHIONED, easy-to-pick lever-tumbler locks (photo 1) can be replaced with modern cylinder type or latch-and-deadbolt locks by cutting out the mortised section and replacing it with a block of solid wood called a Dutchman (photo 2). Taper the cutout and mating block slightly as shown.

Glue the block in place with resorcinol glue, applying pressure with a bar clamp between the strike and hinge edges. The keystone shape transmits clamp pressure to all three sides—which would be impossible with a square insert. No nails or screws are necessary, but if you use them, be sure to set or counterbore so heads are below the wood surface.

The surface of the door can be left as it is or faced with panels (photo 3), depending upon the original thickness of the door into which the new lock is fitted.

BASEMENT WINDOWS are frequently left open during the day for ventilation. Burglars know this and often gain entrance here. Install a Plexiglas shield/vent over the window to increase your security. Form the shield from a single ¼-in. sheet. Make the necessary bends with a strip heater. A homemade strip heater can be made with a Rohm and Haas heating element available at some hardware and most plastic supply outlets. Plans for the heater are provided with the heating element. To install, bore pilot holes for one-way screws in the window frame.

THE STANDARD lock strike is usually light-gauge metal "secured" to a soft-wood jamb with a pair of ½ to ¾-in.-long screws. Installation of a maximum-security strike like this one prevents easy entry.

To install, temporarily remove the doorstop molding to permit routing or chiseling the necessary recess. The doorstop will conceal the long portion of the strike when it's reinstalled. A large hole at the center of the oversize strike allows you to drive a nail through the stop into the jamb to prevent an intruder from using a plastic card to retract a spring-latch type of lock, a favorite technique with burglars.

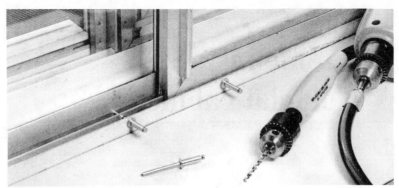

DOOR CHAINS are of limited value when installed with the small screws often supplied with these devices. Note how much larger a screw can be used without reboring the original holes in the hardware. Caution: Chains are secondary locking devices meant only to let you interview a stranger without unlocking door completely.

SLIDING ALUMINUM windows can be opened if a burglar pries apart the typically flimsy framing which usually houses equally-flimsy locks. Drill a hole through the track and window frame to allow insertion of a steel pop rivet. The pop rivet pin locks the sliding panels in a closed-position. Use two rivets at the bottom of each panel. An additional hole in the track will let you leave the window locked but slightly open for ventilation. If window ledge is deep, use a drill bit extension or a flexible shaft to permit drilling close to the edge. Heads of rivets are easy to grip and can be quickly removed from the inside in case of fire or other emergency that requires quick exit.

A PAIR of sturdy screw eyes installed on both sides of a door frame will allow the insertion of a ½-in. steel rod or pipe across the door. This is a simple, positive method of keeping out a lock-picking burglar.

Important: be certain that the bar is easy to remove and allows quick exit in emergency situations. Use at least 3-in.-long screw eyes anchored securely to 2 x 4 door frame members. You should find studs to fasten into between 2 and 5 in. from the edge of the door.

NONRETRACTABLE, one-way screws are often hard to find or not available in the size you require. You can easily make your own screws by filing or grinding two slants as shown above. Rubber or wood pads in the vise will protect screw threads.

Use this type of screw to attach any hardware or ornamentation exposed on the outside of the house, but keep in mind that removal of the hardware will be practically impossible without drilling out the screw or grinding off the screw head.

ENTRANCE DOORS that open to the outside and have removable hinge pins are a welcome sight to burglars. To prevent one from removing the pins and lifting out the door, drill a hole in one hinge leaf and insert a ¼-in.-dia. steel pin. Allow it to protrude about ½ in. Then drill a mating hole through the opposite leaf to receive the protruding pin. The hole should be slightly elongated to provide clearance for the pin as it swings. Add pins to all three of the hinges that hold a typical exterior door.

POLICE STATISTICS indicate that many burglars push in first-floor window airconditioners to gain entry to houses. A ⅛ x ¾-in. steel bar (you can also use ¼ x 1-in. aluminum stock), secured across the top and bottom of the airconditioner with lagscrews, will prevent such break-ins. Windows are rough-framed with double or triple studs, so you can use two 5/16 x 3-in. lagscrews at each end of the brace for a solid grip.

If the design of the airconditioner permits, it's also a good idea to drive screws into the housing to prevent removal to the outside as well.

Safe inside a Colonial cabinet

■ LOOK CAREFULLY around your home, and you will quickly realize that you have many items worth protecting. Electronic equipment, cameras, TV sets and other large items need protection from burglars. But, be aware that you have other possessions that need protection from an even more insidious enemy—fire. By filing valuable papers, deeds, insurance policies and the like in a safe with a fire rating label, you will be assured of having those documents on hand should fire strike your home.

MATERIALS LIST—COLONIAL CABINET

Key	Pcs	Size and Description
A	1	1⅛ x 20-9/16 x 21⅞" pine (top)
B	1	⅜ x ½ x 18⅝" pine (cleat)
C	1	¼ x 19½ x 24" plywood (back)
D	2	¾ x 19 x 24" (side)
E	2	¾ x 1-15/16 x 24" (stile)
F	1	½ x 1⅞ x 20¾" (stop)
G	2	¾ x 2 x 21" (door stile)
H	2	¾ x 2⅛ x 16¼" (door rail)
I	1	¾ x 13 x 17½" (door panel)
J	2	¼ x ½ x 18" (door batten)
K	2	¼ x ½ x 13½" (door batten)

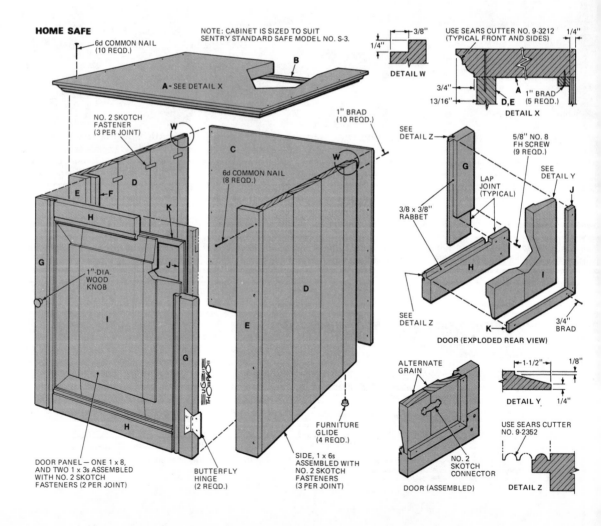

HOME SAFE

NOTE: CABINET IS SIZED TO SUIT SENTRY STANDARD SAFE MODEL NO. S-3.

6d COMMON NAIL (10 REQD.)

A- SEE DETAIL X

B

NO. 2 SKOTCH FASTENER (3 PER JOINT)

W

1" BRAD (10 REQD.)

C

6d COMMON NAIL (8 REQD.)

W

D

E F

K

H

G

J

1"-DIA. WOOD KNOB

I

D

E

G

H

G

DOOR PANEL — ONE 1 x 8, AND TWO 1 x 3s ASSEMBLED WITH NO. 2 SKOTCH FASTENERS (2 PER JOINT)

BUTTERFLY HINGE (2 REQD.)

FURNITURE GLIDE (4 REQD.)

SIDE, 1 x 6s ASSEMBLED WITH NO. 2 SKOTCH FASTENERS (3 PER JOINT)

3/8"
1/4"

DETAIL W

USE SEARS CUTTER NO. 9-3212 (TYPICAL FRONT AND SIDES)
1/4"

3/4"
13/16"
A
D,E
1" BRAD (5 REQD.)

DETAIL X

SEE DETAIL Z

G

5/8" NO. 8 FH SCREW (9 REQD.)

SEE DETAIL Y

LAP JOINT (TYPICAL)

3/8 x 3/8" RABBET

J

H

I

SEE DETAIL Z

K

3/4" BRAD

DOOR (EXPLODED REAR VIEW)

ALTERNATE GRAIN

1-1/2"
1/8"

DETAIL Y
1/4"

USE SEARS CUTTER NO. 9-2352

NO. 2 SKOTCH CONNECTOR

DOOR (ASSEMBLED)

DETAIL Z

To make a safe acceptable in any room, we created this Colonial cabinet with its handsome raised panel door.

Make your cabinet sized to suit your safe. Since the materials for the cabinet should not be too expensive (if you use No. 1 common pine as we did), your total investment for great peace of mind will be reasonable.

Start by cutting the boards to length for sides, top and door panel. Mark the pieces with the letter code (i.e., A, D, I) to avoid mixing the parts. Edges to be butt-joined must be perfectly square, so run the boards through a combination blade on your table saw if they're not. Lay out boards for each section to get the most pleasing grain appearance. Then, flop the boards so they are inside surface up. Apply a light coat of carpenter's aliphatic resin (yellow) glue to mating board edges. Let glue air dry for a few moments, then press board edges together. Permanently fasten boards as shown. Clamp the boards tightly before driving the connectors home. When all boards are joined, there may be a tendency for the section to curl. If so, flop the workpiece, wipe excess glue from joints with a water-dampened cloth and set heavy weights on boards overnight.

The decorative edge on the top's front and side edges is made with a molding cutterhead on the table saw. Push the top through to cut the end grain edges first and finish with the pass for the front edge. The back edge is not shaped. Sand the top smooth, dust and set aside. Next, finish the sides. Check length and width measurements and make sure both sides are identical. Using the table saw, cut the edge rabbets along the back edge of each side to receive the back panel. Cut the front stiles to size and attach to the sides using glue and 6d common nails. Use a stout nailset to set nailheads below the surface. *Do not* fill the nailheads; leave them rough set for an attractive primitive colonial look. Then install part F.

Trim the door insert panel to 13 x 17½ in. and set up your table saw to make the diagonal raised panel cut. Draw the shape (shown in Detail Y) on a piece of scrap lumber and use the scrap to set up your saw fence, blade height and blade angle. Make a test cut on the scrap and, when you're satisfied, set scrap aside. On the door panel make the two endgrain cuts and then the two cuts running with the grain. Next, return blade to 0° setting, and use that test piece of scrap to adjust blade height and fence to make the shoulder cutoff. Run scrap through the saw to be sure settings

FLOOR SAFE WITH CONCRETE JACKET CAN'T BE CARRIED AWAY

TO INSTALL safe, cut hole between joists 2 to 3 in. larger on all sides.

FASTEN metal lath basket to joists with roofing nails.

TAPE LID upside-down to neck of safe and trim off excess tape.

USE STRAIGHT 1 x 3 to screed topping cement level.

BEFORE cement dries, soak up moisture then pull away tape.

DO NOT place door in neck until concrete sets. Keep lock dry.

are correct. When they are, make the cuts on the panel itself. Once again, first do the end-grain passes, then cut with the grain.

Rip the door stiles and rails to width, then, using either router and rabbet cutter, or table saw and two passes, cut the edge rabbet in each member to receive the panel. Next, mount the molding cutterhead on your table saw and shape the inside edges. Finally, after double-checking the panel measurements, cut the lap joints at both ends of stiles and rails. Join the frame members, using glue and ⅝-in. No. 5 fh screws. Install the panel before driving screws home to assure the door remaining square. Hold panel in rabbet with a couple of brads, then lightly apply glue over the joint and conceal it with the ¼-in. batten (J & K) pieces.

Temporarily assemble the cabinet, using scrap strips tacked across the bottom to maintain correct distance between the sides. Tack the top in place and install hinges on the door. Mount the door to the stile and install the knob. (Note: The door on the prototype was created to be a press fit; there is no need for a friction or magnetic catch.) With cabinet assembled, carefully place it over your safe. It should fit with the safe door closed. Double check the cabinet for square and measure for the plywood back. Also measure for the cleat, part B.

Cut the back and disassemble the cabinet. Reassemble the cabinet without the door, using nails and glue. Tack a temporary strip between sides at the cabinet front (nailed to bottoms of sides) to keep the cabinet square while glue sets.

Dust off all wood parts and wipe with a tack rag. On the prototype, we used walnut stain, thinned a bit with turpentine, and tinted slightly with yellow ochre from an art supply dealer. Apply stain, allow it to set at least five minutes, then wipe with a clean, lint-free cloth. Let the cabinet stand for 24 hours.

The next step is to apply a wash coat of 3-lb.-cut white shellac thinned 50 percent with denatured alcohol. Allow shellac to dry at least four hours, then sand it lightly with 180-grit paper. Dust and wipe with a tack rag. Apply one coat of satin-finish varnish. Let it dry at least 48 hours, then rub lightly with 220-grit paper and remove all dust with a tack rag. Add a final coat of satin-finish varnish. When it's dry, mount hinges on the door and door on the cabinet. Install the doorknob.

Before laying out the hole for a floor safe, check to be certain that no cables or pipes under the floor will interfere with your installation.

Make the cuts with a heavy-duty sabre saw, using a tacked-down straightedge as a guide. Next, nail a metal-lath basket to joists and line its inside with 15-lb. felt. Add 1 x 3 frame inside opening, if desired.

Proceed to partially fill the basket with concrete and install the safe with the lid taped on. Level the top of the neck to the existing floor, then fill in around the safe with concrete to ½ in. below the neck top and allow it to set. Finish with topping cement, smooth and level.

BURGLARY PREVENTION THAT DOESN'T COST A CENT

There is a house break-in about every 12 seconds in the United States. By observing a few rules, however, you can lower the odds of your house being the next victim:

■ Before leaving your home, make sure all doors are completely secured.

■ Check seldom-used entrances, such as basement and porch doors, regularly.

■ Check locks on other possible access ways, such as basement vents, skylights and accessible windows.

■ Close your garage door when you leave your home.

■ Keep plantings near windows trimmed so they won't screen intruders.

■ Leave a couple of lights on when you go out in the evening—but not in an obvious spot like the front window.

■ Don't put identifying name tags or addresses on your key sets. They may be picked up by a burglar.

■ When leaving a key for a friend or family member, don't hide it in an obvious spot, like under the doormat or in the mailbox. You should leave it with a trusted neighbor, if possible.

■ Leave only your car ignition key at parking lots and auto repair shops. Lock your glove compartment.

■ Store tools and ladders under lock and key to prevent burglars from using them.

■ Have a locksmith change keys on all locks when you move into a new home.

Going on vacation?

■ Only tell those people who *have* to know about it.

■ Do carloading out of sight of passersby—in the garage or behind the house.

■ Stop all deliveries and have a friend pick up your mail.

■ Ask a neighbor to keep an eye on things.

■ Tell the police; ask them to check your property occasionally.

■ Don't leave your house looking empty or deserted. Draw open all the curtains and blinds slightly.

■ Don't hide valuables in your bedroom, where many burglars look first.

Hide your valuables

■ BURGLARY REMAINS a serious problem everywhere. Security measures, including locks on doors and windows, may not stop the determined housebreaker. Dogs, too, have been known to prove less than effective in confrontation with intruders.

There is a third line of defense, however—and that's what the 10 hiding places shown on these pages are all about. The idea is to outwit the thief by secreting as many of your valuables as possible in unlikely places.

The 10 places shown by no means exhaust the possibilities for subterfuge. Your house or apartment may contain other ideal caches.

Remember, you're matching wits with a potential intruder who has a limited amount of time.

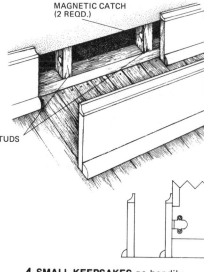

3/4 x 3/4" CLEATS, 4 SIDE

BOTTOM SHELF

3 **SENSIBLE SPOT** for valuables is unde the bottom bookcase shelf. Locate shelf cleats, held with 1¼-in. screws, s the shelf rides just above the unit's base for easy removal. Stock the shelf

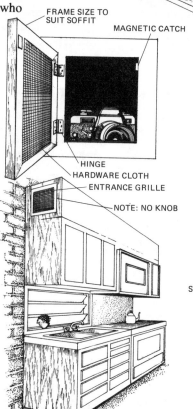

FRAME SIZE TO SUIT SOFFIT

MAGNETIC CATCH

HINGE
HARDWARE CLOTH
ENTRANCE GRILLE
NOTE: NO KNOB

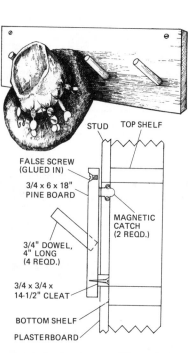

STUD   TOP SHELF

FALSE SCREW (GLUED IN)

3/4 x 6 x 18" PINE BOARD

MAGNETIC CATCH (2 REQD.)

3/4" DOWEL, 4" LONG (4 REQD.)

3/4 x 3/4 x 14-1/2" CLEAT

BOTTOM SHELF

PLASTERBOARD

1 **FAKE HATRACK** hides a hole in the wall for jewelry and other small valuables. Cut between studs, then force-fit 2x4s between them to serve as the header and shelf. The rack rests on a cleat and is held by magnetic catches. A lightweight hat adds credibility to the set-up.

2 **A DOOR** that looks like a vent lets space over cabinets serve as a "safe." Use hinges that don't show. Hold the frame in with magnetic catches and don't use a knob.

MAGNETIC CATCH (2 REQD.)

STUDS

4 **SMALL KEEPSAKES** go handily behind baseboard section. Baseboard height limits available space, so older homes with 1x6 baseboards give the best opportunity here. Magnetic catches hold the "door" in place. Locate furniture to screen baseboard joints from easy view.

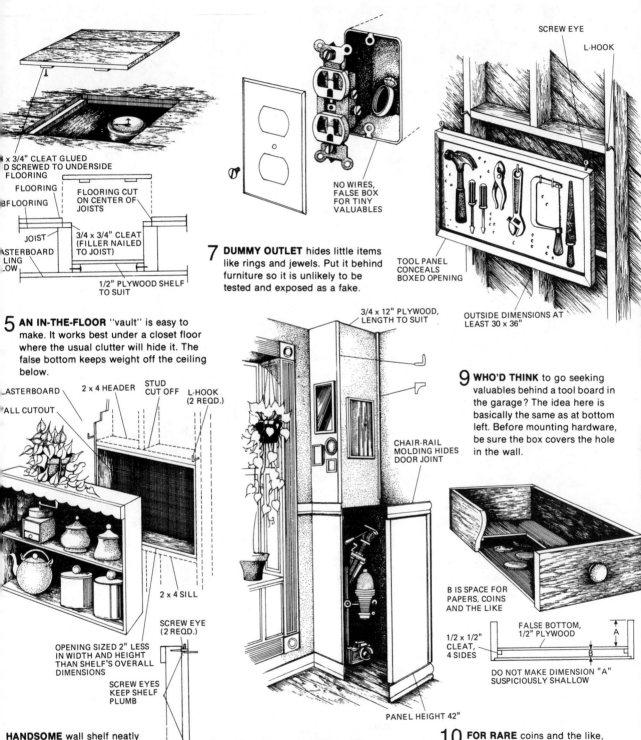

x 3/4" CLEAT GLUED
D SCREWED TO UNDERSIDE
FLOORING

FLOORING
BFLOORING
FLOORING CUT
ON CENTER OF
JOISTS

JOIST
3/4 x 3/4" CLEAT
(FILLER NAILED
TO JOIST)
ASTERBOARD
LING
OW

1/2" PLYWOOD SHELF
TO SUIT

NO WIRES,
FALSE BOX
FOR TINY
VALUABLES

7 DUMMY OUTLET hides little items like rings and jewels. Put it behind furniture so it is unlikely to be tested and exposed as a fake.

SCREW EYE
L-HOOK

TOOL PANEL
CONCEALS
BOXED OPENING

OUTSIDE DIMENSIONS AT
LEAST 30 x 36"

5 AN IN-THE-FLOOR "vault" is easy to make. It works best under a closet floor where the usual clutter will hide it. The false bottom keeps weight off the ceiling below.

ASTERBOARD
ALL CUTOUT

2 x 4 HEADER
STUD
CUT OFF
L-HOOK
(2 REQD.)

3/4 x 12" PLYWOOD,
LENGTH TO SUIT

9 WHO'D THINK to go seeking valuables behind a tool board in the garage? The idea here is basically the same as at bottom left. Before mounting hardware, be sure the box covers the hole in the wall.

CHAIR-RAIL
MOLDING HIDES
DOOR JOINT

2 x 4 SILL

SCREW EYE
(2 REQD.)

OPENING SIZED 2" LESS
IN WIDTH AND HEIGHT
THAN SHELF'S OVERALL
DIMENSIONS

SCREW EYES
KEEP SHELF
PLUMB

B IS SPACE FOR
PAPERS, COINS
AND THE LIKE

FALSE BOTTOM,
1/2" PLYWOOD

1/2 x 1/2"
CLEAT,
4 SIDES

A

B

DO NOT MAKE DIMENSION "A"
SUSPICIOUSLY SHALLOW

HANDSOME wall shelf neatly hides a cutout area. Notice the screw-eyes' location; the bottom pair keeps the box parallel to the wall. Cut the hole first, then build the shelf to ample dimensions to ensure that you will cover the hole completely.

PANEL HEIGHT 42"

8 SMALL APPLIANCES are next to cash and jewels on thieves' hit parade. They'll fit handily in a false corner that looks like a boxed-in chimney. For an easier job, use ¾-in. plywood over 1x3 furring framework. Hide the joints with molding.

10 FOR RARE coins and the like, use space under drawer false bottom. But don't try for too much room, leaving Space A suspiciously shallow. Valuables that might "clink" should be wrapped in sound-deadening material. Solid construction helps, too.

What makes a good house plan?

■ DESIGNING TODAY'S average house requires careful attention to the proper relationship of rooms. The plans of the house shown are an example of good planning.

Starting at the front door, note the small separate entry with its own guest closet. This is in contrast to many front doors, which open directly into the living room. The center hall on the plans shown here leads to the three major rooms as well as the kitchen and family room, eliminating the need to pass through one room to reach another. A case can be made that a center hall wastes space, but the advantages are obvious.

For families that make major use of their living room, a three-exposure space, which in moderate climate would be east, south and west, is best. The formal dining room, not part of the living room, is properly located adjacent to the kitchen. The study occupies its own quiet corner.

Home life today is often centered on the family room. In this plan, the family room is conveniently open to the kitchen with its snack counter. The room should have the morning sun at breakfast time. An important point in kitchen design is the popular practice of outdoor eating and entertaining. Food and drinks can be taken out from the kitchen by way of the back door or from the family room through sliding doors. Guests can reach the patio from the center hall, avoiding the kitchen.

Notice that the lavatory, remote from the activity areas of the house, is privately accessible by both family and guests. This is preferable to one entered from the kitchen or near the front door. Nothing is added to the reserved elegance of a formal gathering by having a guest quietly step out, followed by the sudden rush of water in nearby plumbing.

The first-door laundry in the service area of the house also serves as the traditional back door. Besides being an exit, it is convenient for the home gardener and for children who can wash up in the adjoining lavatory.

The number of daytime living areas you need depends on the activities of your family. You will almost certainly need a kitchen, and laundry, and one or more play areas if you have children. You may also want to have a hobby area, a sewing area, and a quiet work area. Don't forget an area for the family to get together for conversation. Be sure your new house fits the areas you need. Don't buy on bedroom space alone.

A useful characteristic of the plan allows the shopper to return from the market, leave the car either in the driveway or the garage, and bring packages directly into the kitchen. Perhaps with nostalgic thoughts of carriage days and the porte-cochère, a covered walk from driveway to front door would be a nicety for family and guests.

The garage is sized for two cars, with a small amount of storage space at the rear. However, what to do with garden tools, lawn mower, snow blower, bicycles, toys, sleds, summer furniture and more? A larger rear-door shed appended to the garage is almost a present-day necessity. It would dispose of the frequent need to leave one or both cars in the driveway.

Leaving the first floor and going up the open stairway, we find an almost ideally planned sleeping floor with four corner bedrooms. The master bedroom is the largest, with its own bath and generous closets—although ideally this bath would be larger, with two basins, and would be compartmented. Serving the three other bedrooms, with their ample closets, is a second bath. A large linen closet completes the plan.

A primary consideration is the orientation of

FIRST FLOOR

SECOND FLOOR

the house and the climate in which it is located. An example is Charleston, S.C., where many lovingly preserved 18th-century houses are narrow and high-ceilinged, with long two- or three-story piazzas facing east and high narrow windows— all to minimize the hot sun and take advantage of the sea breeze. If there can be one general rule, it is to give the rooms where people will spend most of their time the best exposure.

It has been said that buying a house is the greatest expenditure we'll ever make. What hasn't been said is that we should know as much about buying a house as we often know about buying a car. Maybe the money is best spent on the house that is the best planned.

Beyond an appraisal of a well-planned house, it is helpful to look at some generalized positive factors that contribute to the enjoyment of orderly living.

• A fireplace and chimney located in the interior of a house, as opposed to one in an outside wall, radiate the heat to the surrounding rooms.

• The fireplace located on the long wall of any room allows for a more satisfying furniture grouping.

• Within limits, a small kitchen is most efficient. It saves steps.

• Many families find a breakfast room of greater use than a nook in the kitchen.

• A large cleaning closet in the service area is a must, as is an ample linen closet in the bedroom area.

• With or without air conditioning, bedrooms are more pleasant with windows in two walls, and more so in three. An exception can be a blank wall for privacy.

• A window in a bathroom is always desirable, even with mechanical ventilation.

• A bathroom with both a tub and a stall shower has increased utility.

• Concentrating all the house plumbing results in economy of both installation and use.

• Built-in shelves are a convenience in a bathroom.

• Luxurious as the walk-in closet may be, the walk-in space is really wasted.

• Years ago, many houses were built with the traditional front sitting porch. With the desire for privacy, it gave way to the back porch, often screened. Still later came the patio, and now the deck, made popular by multilevel houses. There is renewed interest, however, in the screened porch, with its rain and insect protection.

• A lovely view should always be exploited.

Outstanding new house plans

■ SELECTING A GOOD house plan is a matter of matching your needs, tastes and lifestyle against the many designs offered. When you study floor plans, remember that they are simply a two-dimensional representation of what will eventually be a three-dimensional reality.

Floor plans are easy to read. Rooms are clearly labeled, with dimensions given in feet and inches. Most symbols are logical and self-explanatory; the location of bathroom fixtures, planters, fireplaces, tile floors, cabinets and counters, sinks, appliances, closets, sloped or beamed ceilings will be obvious.

When you first study a floor plan, imagine that you are walking through the house. By mentally visualizing each room in three dimensions, you can transform the symbols on the plans into something more real.

Start at the front door. It's preferable to have a foyer or entrance hall in which to receive guests. A closet here is desirable; a powder room is a plus.

Look for good traffic circulation as you study the floor plan. You should not have to pass all the way through one main room to reach another. From the entrance area you should have direct access to the three principal areas of a house—the living, work, and sleeping zones.

Study the layout of each zone. Most people expect the living room to be protected from cross traffic. The kitchen, on the other hand, should connect with the dining room—and perhaps also the utility room, basement, garage, patio or deck. You may want the master bedroom near the children, or you may want it as far away as possible. Bathrooms should be convenient to each bedroom—if not adjoining, they should have hallway access and be on the same floor.

Once you are familiar with the layout of the house, look for such structural details as:
• Sufficient uninterrupted wall space for future arrangement.
• Potential heating or cooling problems, such as those you might find in a room over a garage or next to the laundry.

• Window and door placement for good ventilation, natural light and clear views of family outdoor activities.

Every architect commissioned to design a house regretfully remembers the familiar axiom that the perfect plan does not exist. While widespread evidence confirms the fact, informed study can make excellence a realizable goal.

Cape Cod traditional

Deriving its design from the traditional Cape Cod style, this facade features clapboard siding, small-paned windows and a transom-lit entrance flanked by carriage lamps. A central chimney services two fireplaces, one in the country kitchen and the other in the formal living room, which is removed from the disturbing flow of traffic. The master suite is located to the left of the upstairs landing. A full bathroom services two additional bedrooms.

Design PM2657

1,217 Sq. Ft. - First Floor
868 Sq. Ft. - Second Floor
33,260 Cu. Ft.

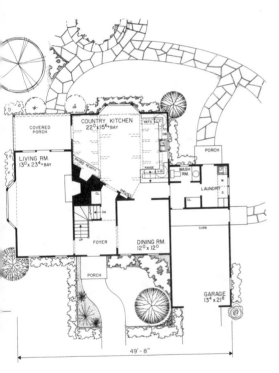

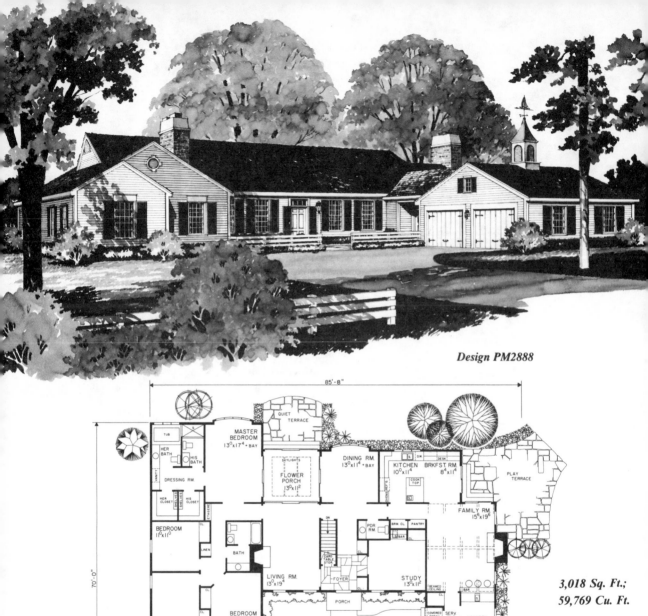

Design PM2888

3,018 Sq. Ft.;
59,769 Cu. Ft.

Early American design for today

This is an outstanding Early American design for the 20th century. The exterior detailing with narrow clapboards, multipaned windows and cupola are the features of yesteryear. Interior planning, though, is for today's active family. Formal living room, informal family room plus a study are present. Every activity will have its place in this home. Picture yourself working in the kitchen. There's enough counter space for two or three helpers. Four bedrooms are in the private area. Stop and imagine your daily routine if you occupied the master bedroom. Both you and your spouse would have plenty of space and privacy. The flower porch, accessible from the master bedroom, living and dining rooms, is a very delightful "plus" feature. Study this design's every detail.

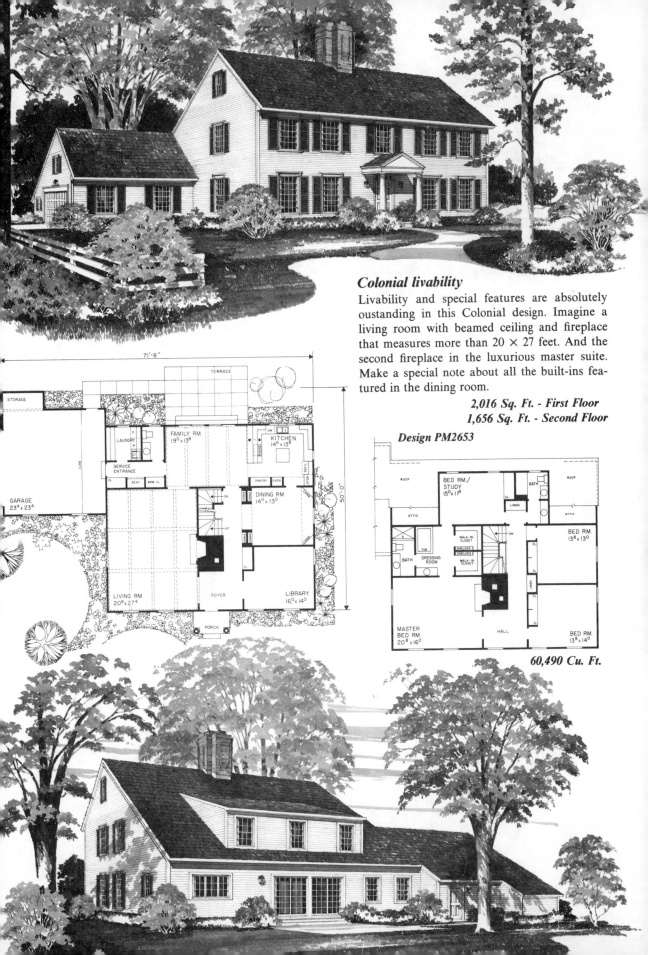

Colonial livability

Livability and special features are absolutely oustanding in this Colonial design. Imagine a living room with beamed ceiling and fireplace that measures more than 20 × 27 feet. And the second fireplace in the luxurious master suite. Make a special note about all the built-ins featured in the dining room.

2,016 Sq. Ft. - First Floor
1,656 Sq. Ft. - Second Floor

Design PM2653

60,490 Cu. Ft.

71'-8"

50'-0"

STORAGE

TERRACE

LAUNDRY

FAMILY RM.
19⁰ x 13⁸

KITCHEN
14⁶ x 13⁸

SERVICE
ENTRANCE

SEAT   BRM CL

PANTRY   OVEN

DINING RM.
14⁰ x 13⁰

GARAGE
23⁴ x 23⁴

DN

LIVING RM.
20⁸ x 27⁴

FOYER

LIBRARY
16⁰ x 14⁰

PORCH

ROOF

BED RM./
STUDY
15⁰ x 11⁸

BATH

ATTIC

LINEN

ROOF

ATTIC

BED RM.
13⁸ x 13⁰

BATH

TUB

DRESSING
ROOM

WALK-IN
CLOSET

SHELVES

SHELVES

WALK-IN
CLOSET

DN

CL

LINEN

MASTER
BED RM.
20⁸ x 16⁰

HALL

BED RM.
13⁸ x 14⁰

1,505 Sq. Ft. - First Floor;
1,344 Sq. Ft. - Second Floor; 45,028 Cu. Ft.

Design PM2610

New England classic

This full two-story traditional will be worthy of note wherever built. It strongly recalls images of a New England of yesteryear. And well it might; for the window treatment is delightful. The front entrance detail is inviting. The narrow horizontal siding and the corner boards are appealing as are the two massive chimneys. The center entrance hall is large with a handy powder room nearby. The study has built-in bookshelves and offers a full measure of privacy. The interior kitchen has a pass-thru to the family room and enjoys all that natural light from the bay window of the nook. A beamed ceiling, fireplace and sliding glass doors are features of the family room. The mud room highlights a closet, laundry equipment and an extra wash room. Study the upstairs with those four bedrooms, two baths and plenty of closets. An excellent arrangement for all.

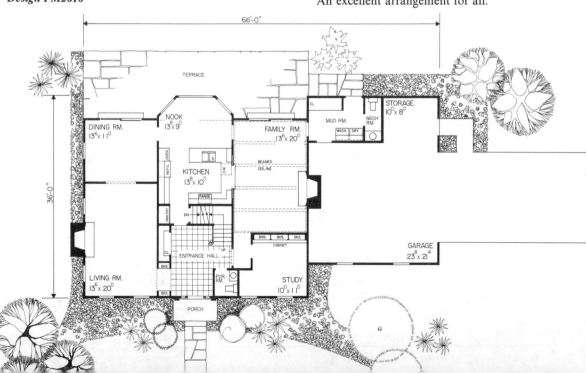

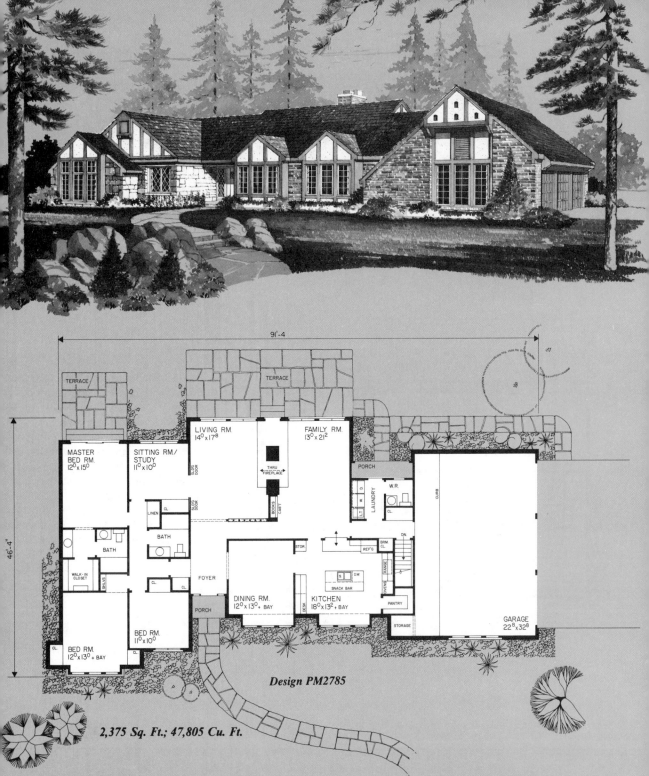

MASTER BED RM. 12⁰ x 15⁰

SITTING RM./ STUDY 11⁰ x 10⁰

LIVING RM. 14⁰ x 17⁸

FAMILY RM. 13⁰ x 21²

THRU FIREPLACE

PORCH

TERRACE

TERRACE

91'-4

46'-4"

LINEN

CL.

BATH

BATH

WALK-IN CLOSET

SHLVS.

CL.

FOYER

PORCH

BED RM. 11⁰ x 10⁰

CL.

CL.

BED RM. 12⁰ x 13⁰ + BAY

DINING RM. 12⁰ x 13⁰ + BAY

DESK

STOR.

KITCHEN 18⁰ x 13² + BAY

SNACK BAR

REF'G

PANTRY

STORAGE

OVENS

RANGE

BRM CL.

DN.

LAUNDRY

W.

D.

W.R.

CL.

CURB

GARAGE 22⁸ x 32⁸

Design PM2785

2,375 Sq. Ft.; 47,805 Cu. Ft.

Tudor inside and out

Exceptional Tudor design! Passers-by will surely take a second glance at this fine home wherever it may be located. And the interior is just as pleasing. As one enters the foyer and looks around, the plan will speak for itself in the areas of convenience and efficiency. Cross room traffic will be avoided. There is a hall leading to each of the three bedrooms and study of the sleeping wing and another leading to the living room, family room, kitchen and laundry with wash room. The formal dining room can be entered from both the foyer and the kitchen. Efficiency will surely be the by-word when describing the kitchen. Note the fine features: a built-in desk, pantry, island snack bar with sink and pass-thru to the family room. The fireplace will be enjoyed in the living and family rooms.

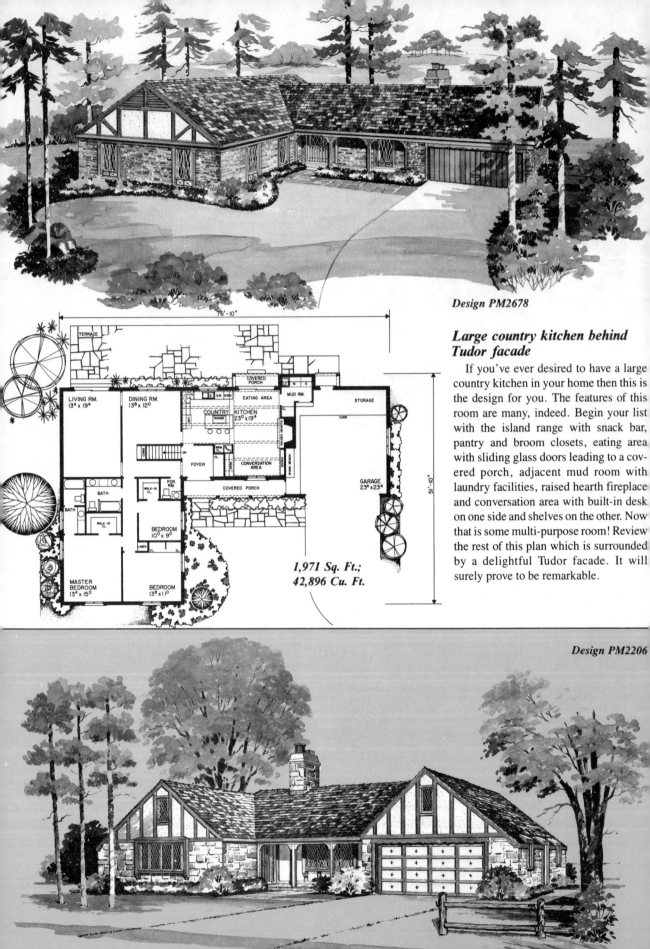

Design PM2678

Large country kitchen behind Tudor facade

If you've ever desired to have a large country kitchen in your home then this is the design for you. The features of this room are many, indeed. Begin your list with the island range with snack bar, pantry and broom closets, eating area with sliding glass doors leading to a covered porch, adjacent mud room with laundry facilities, raised hearth fireplace and conversation area with built-in desk on one side and shelves on the other. Now that is some multi-purpose room! Review the rest of this plan which is surrounded by a delightful Tudor facade. It will surely prove to be remarkable.

76'-10"

51'-10"

TERRACE

LIVING RM.
13⁴ x 19⁴

DINING RM.
13⁸ x 12⁰

COVERED PORCH

EATING AREA

MUD RM.

W D

STORAGE

COUNTRY KITCHEN
23⁰ x 19⁴

RANGE

CURB

FOYER

CONVERSATION AREA

GARAGE
23⁴ x 23⁴

BATH

BATH

WALK-IN CL.

PDR. RM.

WALK-IN CL.

BEDROOM
10⁰ x 9⁰

COVERED PORCH

LINEN

MASTER BEDROOM
13⁴ x 15⁰

BEDROOM
13⁸ x 11⁰

**1,971 Sq. Ft.;
42,896 Cu. Ft.**

Design PM2206

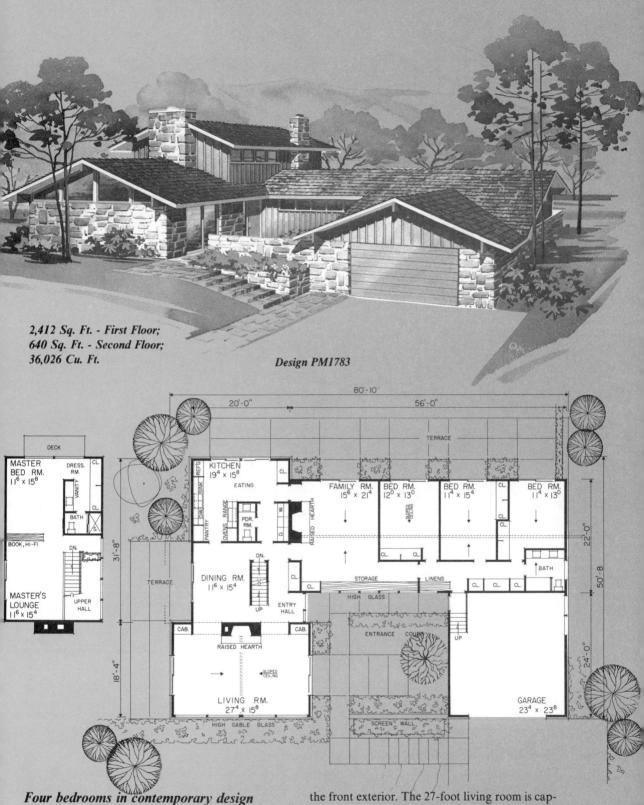

2,412 Sq. Ft. - First Floor;
640 Sq. Ft. - Second Floor;
36,026 Cu. Ft.

Design PM1783

Floor Plan Labels

DECK

MASTER BED RM.
11⁶ x 15⁸

DRESS. RM.

CL.

VANITY

CL.

BATH

BOOK, HI-FI

DN.

MASTER'S LOUNGE
11⁶ x 15⁴

UPPER HALL

80'-10"

20'-0"

56'-0"

TERRACE

KITCHEN
19⁴ x 15⁸

CL.

EATING

REFG

SINK

DW.

FAMILY RM.
15⁶ x 21⁴

BED RM.
12⁰ x 13⁰

BED RM.
11⁴ x 15⁴

BED RM.
11⁴ x 13⁰

PANTRY

OVENS

RANGE

PDR. RM.

W.

D.

RAISED HEARTH

CL.

SLOPING CEILING

CL.

31'-8"

22'-0"

TERRACE

DINING RM.
11⁶ x 15⁴

DN.

CL.

STORAGE

LINENS

CL.

CL.

CL.

BATH

UP

HIGH   GLASS

50'-8"

ENTRY HALL

CAB.

RAISED HEARTH

CAB.

ENTRANCE COURT

UP

18'-4"

SLOPED CEILING

LIVING RM.
27⁴ x 15⁸

SCREEN   WALL

GARAGE
23⁴ x 23⁸

24'-0"

HIGH GABLE GLASS

Four bedrooms in contemporary design

Large families, take notice! Here is an impressive contemporary that is not only going to be fun to live in, but to look at as well. Contributing to the appeal of this design are the interesting roof levels, their exposed rafters and wide overhangs. A big entrance court, screened from the street by a masonry wall, heightens the drama of the front exterior. The 27-foot living room is captivating, indeed. It can function through sliding glass doors, with either the front court or the side terrace. Eating patterns can be quite flexible with the extra space in the kitchen, a formal dining room, and also a dining terrace. Don't miss sloping ceilings which are throughout this contemporary plan.

2,583 Sq. Ft. - First Floor;
697 Sq. Ft. - Second Floor;
51,429 Cu. Ft.

Design PM1228

French Regency tradition

This beautiful house has a wealth of detail taken from the rich traditions of French Regency design. The roof itself is a study in pleasant dormers and the hips and valleys of a big flowing area. A close examination of the plan shows the careful arrangement of space for privacy as well as good circulation of traffic. The spacious formal entrance hall sets the stage for good zoning. The informal living area is highlighted by the updated version of the old country kitchen. Observe the fireplace, and the barbecue. While there is a half-story devoted to the master bedroom suite, this home functions more as a one-story country estate design than as a 1½ story.

2,341 Sq. Ft. - Main Level;
1,380 Sq. Ft. - Lower Level; 51,290 Cu. Ft.

Design PM2846

66'-0"

DECK

FAMILY RM.
12⁰ x 17⁶

KITCHEN
11⁰ x 16⁰

DINING RM.
11⁴ x 14⁰

LIVING RM.
16⁰ x 17⁶

COVERED PORCH

MASTER BEDROOM
13⁸ x 15⁰

OVEN

BRM. CL.

PANTRY

OPEN OVER PLANTER

BEDROOM
12⁰ x 11²

FOYER

PDR. RM.

LINEN

WALK-IN CLOSET

CL.

LINEN   TUB

BATH

COVERED PORCH

STUDY
12⁰ x 12⁰

BATH

BEDROOM
12⁰ x 11⁴

LAUNDRY

OPEN ABOVE

OPEN ABOVE

OPEN ABOVE

COURT

CURB

GARAGE
23⁴ x 22⁰

COVERED TERRACE

LOUNGE
22⁶ x 17⁶

GUEST BEDROOM
11⁶ x 14⁰

BASEMENT

UNEXCAVATED

AIR COND.

SNACK BAR

SUMMER KITCHEN
14⁸ x 9⁸

STORAGE

BATH

LINEN

UNEXCAVATED

HOBBIES / SHOP

GAMES RM.
21⁸ x 15⁰

Spanish split-level design

The street view of this Spanish design shows a beautifully designed onestory home, but now take a look at the rear elevation. This home has been designed to be built into a hill so the lower level can be opened to the sun.

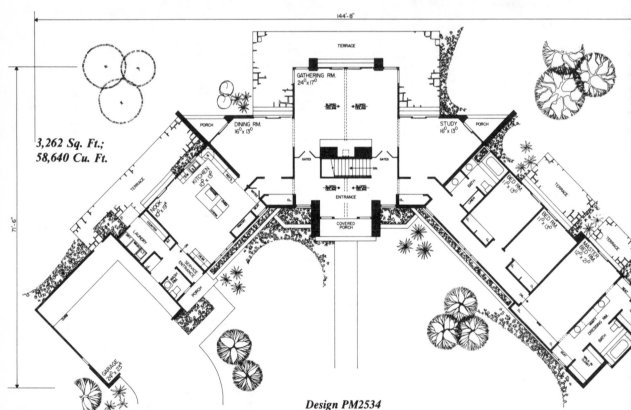

Design PM2534

Ranch design with rambling wings

The angular wings of this ranch home surely contribute to the unique character of the exterior. These wings effectively balance what is truly a dramatic and inviting front entrance. Massive masonry walls support the wide overhanging roof with its exposed wood beams. The patterned double front doors are surrounded by delightful expanses of glass. The raised planters and the masses of quarried stone (make it brick if you prefer) enhance the exterior appeal. Inside, a dis-

tinctive and practical floor plan stands ready to shape and serve the living patterns of the active family. The spacious entrance hall is highlighted by sloped ceilings and an attractive open stairway to the lower level recreation area. An impressive fireplace and an abundance of glass are features of the big gathering room. Interestingly shaped dining room and study flank this main living area. The large kitchen offers many of the charming aspects of the family-kitchen of yesteryear. The master bedroom suite is sunken.

How to spot a good house

■ WHEN YOU BUY A HOUSE, you make the single largest purchase of your lifetime—so in this, of all purchases, you should be a wise buyer. Yet too many people buy a house with less investigation than if they were buying a new TV or a used car.

How does one become a good house buyer? The average family buys from one to three homes in a lifetime, not enough to become ex-

WHEN BUYING a new house, visit other homes being constructed by the builder, where you can see how they are built.

SPOTTING a good house begins with a check of nearby lots, to see that there is favorable water drainage. Next, look at the design of the house and how it relates to the lot. Then inspect the exterior. If you are satisfied up to this point, then start an investigation of the interior layout and condition.

perienced house hunters. Furthermore, home purchases often are made under pressure. Buyers may have only a few weeks to shop because of a transfer, or because they sold a house they must vacate by a specified date.

And there are so many considerations beyond the condition of their new house: neighborhood, proximity to shopping, transportation and schools.

Most people worry about price when buying a house, yet price is one of the easier problems to solve. You know how much money you have for a down payment. You soon learn how much mortgagors will loan on a house, and how much the monthly payments will be. These factors set the limits on your purchase. The real problem is one of finding a good house that fits your family's lifestyle within the boundaries set by money.

No matter how much you have to spend, you should be able to get a good house for your dollars by knowing what to look for and what to avoid.

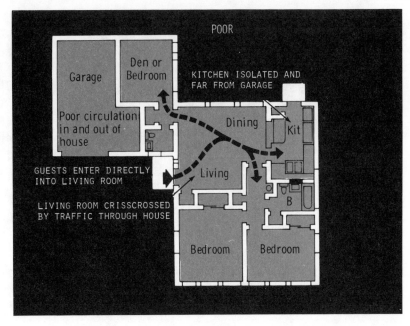

A GOOD FLOOR PLAN is as important as good construction because it affects your daily life. Look for good separation of living, working and sleeping areas. Bedrooms should be shielded from entertaining areas. You should be able to go from one room to another without passing through a third room. The plan at the near right is poor because all traffic must criss-cross through the living room. Both plans at the far right work well because they permit good traffic flow and there is separation between the living and sleeping areas. Other items to check: The kitchen should be near the garage; some type of entrance hall should be provided; bathroom should be located near bedrooms; and there should be easy access to the house from the front.

Ask yourself these questions when buying a house, old or new:

1. Does the house have an attractive appearance? Is it well-situated on the lot, with a good house-to-site relationship?

2. Does it have a livable floor plan? Does traffic move through it sensibly, and are the different living areas well separated?

3. How good are the major appliances, including the furnace, water heater, sump pump, and laundry and kitchen appliances? How old are

they? Are they reliable units with recognized brand names?

4. What type of electrical service is supplied, and how good is the wiring?

5. How well is the house constructed?

6. Has the basement (if any) ever flooded?

If you know the answers to these questions, the chances of buying a bad house are cut considerably.

Appearance. A good house is set on the lot to take advantage of the best view or best exposure

IMPORTANCE OF A SOUTHERN exposure for main living areas is shown below. With sun low in winter, you take advantage of its light and heat. In summer, sun is high and is usually blocked by roof overhang.

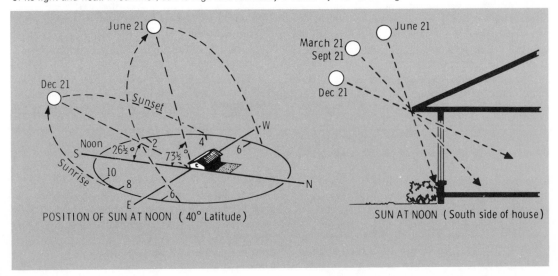

POSITION OF SUN AT NOON (40° Latitude)

SUN AT NOON (South side of house)

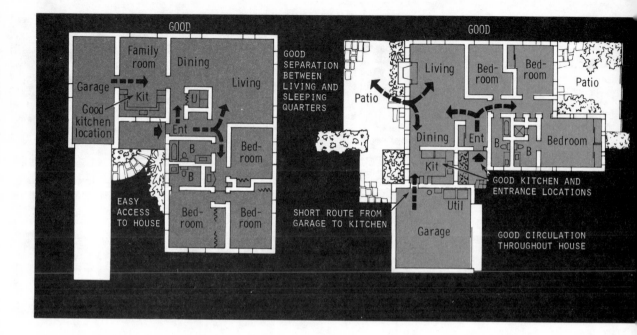

in relation to the sun and prevailing winds. A southern exposure usually is best. It is the only one that lets warm sunshine into your house all winter. This means bright, pleasant rooms and lower heating bills.

South windows are easy to shade with deciduous trees, which lose their leaves in the winter to let the sun through; by awnings; or by deep roof overhangs, which allow the lower-angled winter sun in when you need it.

Not all houses, of course, can face south. This is where the design of the house becomes important. Though it may face a street to the east or west, the house can be designed with big windows in the side with the best view, and it can be oriented to the south side. A poorly designed house, for example, might have many windows in the north side and few on the south.

Stand outside and visualize the effect of the sun on the house, keeping in mind windows and placement of trees. How will the sun affect the house in the summer? In the winter? The side of the house facing the prevailing wind and storm track will take the brunt of driving rains and winter winds. Is it sheltered by trees? Does it have too many windows? Are there storm windows? If there is an entrance on this side, is it sheltered in some way?

Ordinarily, a house should be set forward on its lot to give you the most land at the back for your private use. As you look at a house and lot,

mentally divide the grounds into three main areas: public, private and service.

The *public* area is the front lawn. The *private* area, screened from public view by the house and landscaping, is the part for outdoor living. The *service* zone consists of the driveway, and areas for trash cans and outdoor equipment storage.

A large public area is a disadvantage because you must maintain it for the sake of appearance, yet you get very little practical use from it. At the same time, this area is vital to the overall appearance of the house, for a skimpy public area reduces the apparent size of the house.

A large private area means you can do more outdoor living. Look for patios, screened porches, cookout and garden areas on the private side of the house.

When looking at service areas, look for adequacy and convenience. The service areas should be screened from those areas used for outdoor living.

Finally, consider water drainage around the house. Can storm water drain away from the house? The natural slope of the lot and nearby land should carry rain water away from the foundation. Be wary of homes in low spots which receive drainage from adjacent areas. The best house location is one which is higher than other nearby land, and which is graded for good water runoff.

House-to-site relationship. Look at the house from the front. Does it seem to stick up out of the ground? Or does it blend into the lot—part of a unified whole? Part of this is good landscaping and part is the way the house is built on the lot. Decide whether improved landscaping might improve the house-to-site relationship. If so, don't forget to add the cost of new landscaping to your house budget.

Types of houses. You'll find single-story homes; the story-and-a-half house; the two and three-story house; and the split-level house. Each has advantages and disadvantages.

You won't have stairs to climb in the one-story house. It is easier to maintain, both inside and out, and items like painting and roof repairs cost less.

The one-story house allows the most flexible floor planning, but not all one-story houses are well planned. Look for good room zoning—good separation between the living, working and sleeping zones.

The story-and-a-half house isn't often built today, but thousands have been put up over the years. The house is basically designed for living on the first floor, with the attic space sometimes finished to provide additional bedrooms.

Check the attic in these. If unfinished, you should see good insulation under the roof. If finished, find out how well it was insulated during finishing. These houses can get extremely hot under the roof because ventilation is usually provided only by small dormer windows.

A two-story house gives a feeling of size and permanence. You get the most house on the least land for the least cost per square foot. It offers natural separation between downstairs living activities and upstairs sleeping areas.

Two-story houses are easier to heat than spread-out ranch homes because heat rises. Downstairs rooms are cooler in the summer, while upstairs rooms may be quite hot. Check the insulation of the roof and mark it as a plus if the house has a ventilating fan in the ceiling of the second-floor hall (even if the house is centrally air-conditioned).

Maintenance of a two-story house is difficult. Exterior painting requires long ladders and some spots near the top may be hard to reach. Roof and gutter repairs can be difficult, even hazardous.

The split-level house combines some of the advantages of one and two-story houses. It offers a natural division of living zones, but it also has stairs. However, you won't do as much stair

KEEP A SHARP EYE out for the use of top-grade materials in a house. Here, you can see good hardwood parquet flooring, an indication of quality construction. Don't be misled, however, by eye-catching features such as luminous ceiling or kitchen pass-throughs which may divert your attention from poor materials.

climbing as in a two-story. Check these houses for good insulation in the lowest and highest levels. The lowest levels are partially below grade, and therefore may be subject to flooding and moisture problems. If the foundation was sealed and the walls were insulated, these problems are minimized. But rainwater drainage could be a problem.

As you examine the house (or any house), look for evidence of flooding: high-water marks on basement walls; equipment such as washers on platforms off the floor; and non-use of the basement for storage. If the basement is freshly painted, be wary. The paint may hide high-water marks.

The split-level house is best on a sloping lot, where it fits into the contours of the land. Sometimes, split-level homes are stuck on dead-level lots. Unless earth has been brought in to grade these places, they look like displaced persons on the land.

Floor plans. The keys to any floor plan are easy access to all rooms, good separation of the living zones, and a traffic pattern that is easy to live with.

When you enter a house, ideally you should be able to go straight to every room without passing through another room. If you must pass through a room, count it as one demerit. If you must go through the living room to get to the kitchen or to a stairway, score a double demerit.

Does the back door enter directly into the kitchen, or into a utility or mud room? Entry through a utility room will save a lot of kitchen clean-up.

One way to evaluate a house is to think of day and night areas. A house with four bedrooms may sleep your family comfortably—but what happens when everyone is up and active? Look over the house to see how many separate daytime activity areas there are.

A combined living room and dining room counts as one daytime space. A family room is one space. A combined kitchen-family room may be one space or two, depending on the layout.

How many daytime living areas do you need? This depends on your family. Almost all families need a kitchen, a laundry area, and perhaps sewing, work or hobby areas. Children of different age groups may have to be divided for afternoon play, and this calls for separate areas. Count up the areas that you need, then see that your new house fits. Don't just buy on bedroom space alone.

The kitchen deserves critical attention. Look for a good ''work triangle''—the arrangement of the refrigerator, sink and range. Measure the distance from the work spot in front of the range to the refrigerator door, and from the refrigerator door to the sink, and then back to the range. Add up the total running feet. According to research at Cornell University's Kitchen Laboratory, the minimum footage should be 12 to 15, the maximum 22. Anything less than 12 feet will be crowded; more than 22 feet will require too much walking.

Look for plenty of countertop space. The University of Illinois Small Homes Council recommends at least 4½ ft. of countertop on the open side of the refrigerator door, between the refrigerator and the sink; 3½ to 4 ft. between the sink and the range; and at least 2 ft. on the other side of the range. These are minimums. The Council also suggests a minimum of 8½ running feet of wall cabinets, plus at least 20 cu. ft. of storage under the counters.

Grade a house, too, on the location of its bathrooms. There should be a full bath near the bedrooms, and for greatest convenience, a full bath for each two bedrooms. Look for a powder room in the living area of a ranch house, or on the first floor of a multi-storied house.

Appliances. Are the range, oven, dishwasher and disposal unit built in? Find out how old they are and how well they work. You may face repair bills in the near future. Don't pass up a house when everything is good but the appliances are old. Just add the cost of possible appliance replacement to the cost of the house.

The same is true of the furnace, air-conditioning equipment, hot water heater, and the laundry units. All can be replaced, and indeed someday must be replaced. The real question is how much use you will get out of them before replacement. You don't want to face a large replacement expense on top of a new mortgage unless you are prepared for it.

Brand-name appliances are important because you have a better chance of getting service and replacement parts.

Electric power. This is a major consideration. Our use of electrical appliances has increased by astounding leaps in recent years. Homes which were adequately wired 10 years ago often can't handle the load of appliances a family puts to use today.

Ask the following questions about electric power service:

1. Is it two-wire or three-wire? (It should be three-wire.)

2. Is it 60-ampere service, 100-ampere service, 150-ampere service? At one time, 3-wire 60-amp service was considered adequate. Today, 3-wire 100-amp service is a bare minimum. If you have a workshop, look to 150-amp service as adequate. Get the answers to these questions from the power company, and if power is inadequate, find how much it will cost to increase the service. Do this now, before you buy the house.

3. How many circuits? You should have one lighting circuit employing a 15-amp fuse for each 500 sq. ft. of living area. In addition, you should have two 20-amp appliance circuits in the kitchen, breakfast area and dining room. Laundry equipment, the garbage disposer and the electric range should be on their own separate circuits.

Look at the main electric service box and count the number of fuses or circuit breakers. The use of fuses indicates older wiring. If you see circuit breakers, the work was done more recently—but still may not be adequate.

Check gas and electric bills. These tell you much about how well the house is insulated and the annual upkeep costs. If the electric bill is lower than your present bill, think again about the wiring of the house. You apparently need more electricity than the present occupants.

House construction and condition. If you are buying a new house, you may see it under construction, or see what the contractor is building into nearby houses. If you are considering an older house, you'll have to hunt for clues to good construction. Here are some features to look for:

1. *Foundation walls* of poured concrete usually are better than cinder or concrete-block walls. Block walls should be plastered with ½-in. of cement mortar on the outside. In high-quality construction they are reinforced with steel.

2. *Troweled-on waterproofing* is better than the brushed or sprayed-on type.

3. *Drain tile* installed at the base of the foundation walls gets rid of ground water that otherwise may get into the basement.

4. *Exterior walls* on a new house should have a primer and two finish coats of top-quality paint. If you are looking at an old house, find out when it was last painted. Depending on weather, paint quality and other factors, you'll have to paint every three to six years.

5. *Interior walls* may be lath-and-plaster or gypsum wallboard. As the house settles, lath-and-plaster is more subject to cracking. On the other hand, in skimpy construction thin ⅜-in. wallboard is too often used. This damages easily and allows transmission of noise. Wallboard should be at least ½-in. thick, and preferably ⅝-in. The best wallboard construction consists of two layers of board, the first nailed to the studs and the second cemented to the first.

6. *Flooring*, if it will be seen, should be hardwood, preferably oak, smoothly installed. Often, in kitchens and in rooms which will be carpeted, no hardwood is installed. Instead, a subfloor of plywood is put down, and the floor covering laid over it. There is no point in paying for hardwood you will never see.

The floor of the kitchen gets a lot of wear, and present-day kitchen floor coverings are both durable and beautiful, and offer easy care. If the floor is relatively new, count it as a plus. If it is quite old, figure on replacing it.

7. *Windows and doors*, in more severe climates, should be weatherstripped and have storm installations. In older houses, check for looseness and for windows which won't open.

8. *Kitchen counters* should have a durable surface, preferably a plastic laminate or ceramic tile.

9. *Electric outlets* should be well distributed throughout the house. The National Electric Code calls for an outlet every 12 feet of wall space, and a switched light, operated from a switch near the door, for every room. Check the kitchen for two separate 20-amp circuits strictly for appliance use.

10. *Bathrooms* should have waterproof walls and floors. The best are finished in ceramic tile. Plastic tile and hardboard tile panels also are used. Areas around the sink and tub should be tiled. Look for good quality electric and plumbing fixtures, with recognized brand names on them. An enameled cast-iron tub is considered top quality, preferably with a shower enclosure. Avoid plastic tubs.

Bathroom faucets should be made of brass coated in chrome or nickel. Look to see that they don't drip or leak, that they turn easily, and that sink and tub drains work properly. Flush the toilets to check the noise and the flushing action.

Plumbing is difficult to check. Turn on a water faucet to check pressure and rate of flow. If it is slow, be wary. The town may have low water pressure. More likely, the water pipes are too small or they are becoming clogged with lime deposits.

There should be a shutoff valve for every water fixture in the house. Listen for "water hammer" as you turn the faucets on and off. This banging noise is easily cured by installing standpipes in the system, but you have to pay the plumber. Add another cost item to the price of the house.

11. *The water heater* must be large enough for your family. Thirty-gallon types are seldom sufficient. Look for 40 gallons or more in gas-heated units, and 80 gallons in electric units. Good water heaters are guaranteed for 10 years or more. Ask when this water heater was installed.

12. *Asphalt shingles* on the roof should be of the 235-lb. type and should be sealed down with glue tabs to prevent wind damage. Look the present roof over for signs of wear—thin spots in the surface coating, crumbling edges, broken shingles. If wood shakes or other roofing was used, inspect to see that none are missing and that all are well-anchored.

Many people have decided to buy old houses with the idea of updating them. They feel they can get a good buy because of the condition of the house.

Under the right circumstances, this can be a good way to get a good house—but not cheap. If the house is basically sound, but needs such things as a new heating plant, new electric wiring, or new plumbing, you can expect a very hefty expense. If you are tempted to follow this route, pay an electrician, a plumber or a heating contractor to give you an estimate on the new work *before* you decide to buy. Your mind may suddenly be changed.

Also, in looking at very old houses, remember that in the old days, bathrooms were few and kitchens came equipped with a sink—period. Putting in new bathrooms and bringing an old kitchen up to date are expensive chores.

Many people hope to offset the cost by doing the work themselves. Experience shows that in very old houses, much of the work is so difficult that you end up with professional crews.

Things to look for in a very old house. These include wet basements, no drains in basement floors, doors and windows which stick because of excessive settling, ancient electric wiring, old and clogged plumbing, a tired heating system, absolute lack of insulation, signs of termites or termite damage, worn-out gutters, worn-out roof, worn-out water heater, and a general sagging of the house.

Be cautious of a house which has settled too much and sags. Restructuring a place like this is very expensive. If you see evidence of termites, find out how much damage has been done before you buy. You could be facing a large rebuilding bill.

Check the tilt of floors, the leans and curves of walls. These often mean that the house is in real trouble.

The right way to go after an old, old house is to check it for basic soundness. When satisfied that it sits well on its foundation and has no major problems, make a list of essential remodeling, including wiring, heating, plumbing, insulation, etc. Don't kid yourself as you compile the list. If the place needs the work, put it on the list—and don't assume you can do it all yourself.

Now get good estimates of the work, and then add this total to the price asked for the house. The new figure is the real price you may be paying for the house, even though it may take you a couple of years to pay it all out.

Does the house still look like a good buy? Make one other check. Find out what other houses in the neighborhood are selling for. Get some idea of what your house would be worth after the remodeling was done. You may find that you won't ever be able to get your money out of the place.

On the other hand, you may find that it's a great buy!

BY THE TIME you see the termite tunnels such as these, hidden damage is terribly extensive. The insects were at work a long time here.

THIS BATHROOM looks great, but poor workmanship can cost you plenty. The pipes here leaked, and the whole floor had to be replaced.

Building codes

■ BUILDING CODES can be the homeowner's best friend. Followed in new home construction, they guarantee the buyer that workmanship and materials conform to the most recent testing by manufacturers and the years of experience of qualified builders. For the do-it-yourselfer about to engage in a remodel, building codes provide guidelines and assistance in planning and construction to assure work will be both safe and long-lasting.

Codes are the result of product testing combined with building experience shaped into rules for procedures known to work and last. These codes assure you'll get plumbing that doesn't leak or smell; electrical wiring that can't shock or burn; and construction that will safely support a structure and use the latest engineering knowledge about materials.

It is false economy to circumvent the code and inspection process because of the cost in fees or the possibilities of reassessment leading to higher taxes. Inferior materials and short-cut workmanship only seem a bargain in the beginning. As walls crumble or crack, fuses blow, roofs leak or plumbing backs up, the necessities of regulation will become clear.

Today it is easy to do things right. Most lumberyards or home supply stores sell products that have been factory-engineered to code requirements. The salespeople generally know what you need to be compatible with the code for most situations. Study the project at home before you begin. When your job puzzles you, help is nearby. Building codes are always available to the general public to read and study. In some towns, they are kept at public libraries in addition to the building department offices in City Hall.

Your secret helper—the building inspector

Every town has a building department, with a staff drawn from experienced former tradespeople. You should always discuss your project with these officials before you begin to buy materials. Frequently, local building ordinances have special requirements based on the conditions in your town. These procedures may differ from or expand state or national codes. And the only way is the right way for where you live. The building inspector can suggest the specific materials to purchase and tell you how best to install them. If you arrange for inspections, you will gain the security of knowing you did everything right. In some cases, if problems occur in uninspected work, your house insurance will be void and no claims will be paid.

Electrical codes

Electrical wiring procedures are extremely important to follow precisely. Shock or fire can result from ignorance or shoddy workmanship. In any wet location, such as bathrooms or basements, because of grounded water pipes and wet surfaces, electrical problems there could be fatal. Yet household wiring is not really very complicated, and the code will tell you just how things should be done: Lights are generally built into wall outlets or ceilings with only a switch or two per room; wall outlets can accommodate normal appliances.

Adding another circuit, or troubleshooting a problem, is simplified by standard code procedures. To prevent shocks in any wet area, electrical codes require the installation of ground fault circuit interrupters (GFCI). These devices turn off any electrical line automatically and instantly if the slightest overload is sensed. The GFCI can be wired into a circuit either as a breaker at the main panel or as the receptacle at each outlet. Kitchen counters require double outlets every four linear feet, and these outlets must be supplied by at least two circuits. Rather than a nuisance, this rule means there will be enough places to plug in coffee makers or food processors, with sufficient power to avoid household blackouts or overheat wiring hidden in the walls. Outdoor wiring for porch lights, illuminated walkways or patio outlets must be in special waterproof housings. These are just some of the ways that the electrical rules in the building code make our homes safer and easier to live in.

Plumbing codes

Plumbing codes were developed to prevent disease or nasty smells and to assure the efficient supply of water and removal of waste. In the simple cases, this means that fixtures must be mounted with traps and shutoffs, and that plumbing lines must be slanted downward. Your plumbing inspector can tell you exactly what to do in any situation.

If your intended project is remodeling, plan for maintenance in the future. Change or replace any plumbing parts that are not in excellent condition. Add shutoff valves to every water line supplying any fixture. Many older houses were plumbed with only one water shutoff, usually located in a dark corner of the basement or in a vault in the yard. Modern plumbing code requires valves by the end use point of every line, so you don't have to run to the basement to change a washer in the third floor bath.

Plastic pipe is a good material to use where it is permitted by code. Plastic pipe requires fewer tools to work, is easy and quicker to install by the do-it-yourselfer, and will last many times the life of metal pipes. Most codes, however, now only allow it for waste drain lines. Check with your local building official.

In your remodel, plumbing expense and trouble will be minimized if you don't have to move any pipes. If possible, retain fixtures in the same location. When you reuse a tub or sink, you save the cost of a new one and the effort of replumbing it. On the other hand, your kitchen may not have a new look and better utility unless you do swap the old sink for a new one. Just attempt to use the same drain and supply lines where that works. Be sure that new work uses any new improvements as specified by plumbing codes.

Save water. Install flow restrictor washers in faucets and showerheads, or switch to new units with water-saving design. Older fixtures use much more water than is required. Waste costs you money in energy to heat and money for the water itself. It also burdens sewage disposal systems. And toilets designed to use as much as 60% less water are now available from quality manufacturers.

Construction codes

Building codes are specific about materials to use wherever there is construction. These rules are designed to make any structure strong, watertight and resistant to decay or deterioration. Codes specify the optimum number and spacing of studs in a wall and minimum sizes for various types of lumber. If there are better ways to apply roofing and flashing, the code will suggest them. Ventilation openings and moisture barriers will be specified where needed. In areas where there is earthquake or other natural dangers, codes will have extra requirements to make your home safe.

Building rules will help protect your home from shoddy materials by specifying the type, size and number of different building supplies. It will also state what type of nail or screw should be used, and just how many should be used to guarantee sufficient strength. Code will require water resistant construction materials whenever possible. Plywood for walls or floors should be exterior grade because it is made with waterproof glue. It will resist delamination if any leaks do occur. Any plasterboard for bathrooms or wet areas must be the water-resistant type, easily identified by its greenish surface.

Lack of proper ventilation is the cause of most rot or decay problems in older houses. Accumulated moisture can become rot in floor or wall members. Building codes now take these factors into account, and can stipulate different types of house ventilation. Most common needs are found in kitchens, baths, attics and basements.

In the bathroom, people close doors and windows when they bathe or shower, causing moisture to accumulate. Boiling water and cooking steam condense on kitchen surfaces. Built-in vents with automatic fans connected to the outside can dissipate the moisture and dramatically improve the life of a kitchen or bathroom. In the attic, the utility of insulation will be damaged if water vapor cannot escape. Code suggests the proper amount of eve, ridge or soffit venting for any situation. Basements that are damp will mildew or rust stored items and could stimulate rot in structural members. Code requirements will avoid these problems in new construction and may be able to correct these problems in a remodel project.

Concrete, foundation and reinforcement code

The longevity of any structure will be determined in part by the quality of the basic foundation. To protect the homeowner, building codes examine and specify exactly what should be provided for any type of construction. That means the regulation of the process from the type and quality of cement block or concrete as the foundation material to the method of sizing for form work and the amount and type of steel provided for reinforcement.

Block construction is different from poured concrete, and both have specific requirements. Concrete must have the correct proportions of cement, sand and gravel to be as strong as stone.

These rules will make certain the materials are correct. Inspections by the building officials during stages of construction will guarantee the quality of work in that project.

SHOP GUIDE

CUSTOMARY TO METRIC (CONVERSION)
Conversion factors can be carried so far they become impractical. In cases below where an entry is exact it is followed by an asterisk (*). Where considerable rounding off has taken place, the entry is followed by a + or a − sign.

Linear Measure

inches	millimeters
1/16	1.5875*
1/8	3.2
3/16	4.8
1/4	6.35*
5/16	7.9
3/8	9.5
7/16	11.1
1/2	12.7*
9/16	14.3
5/8	15.9
11/16	17.5
3/4	19.05*
13/16	20.6
7/8	22.2
15/16	23.8
1	25.4*

inches	centimeters
1	2.54*
2	5.1
3	7.6
4	10.2
5	12.7*
6	15.2
7	17.8
8	20.3
9	22.9
10	25.4*
11	27.9
12	30.5

feet	centimeters	meters
1	30.48*	.3048*
2	61	.61
3	91	.91
4	122	1.22
5	152	1.52
6	183	1.83
7	213	2.13
8	244	2.44
9	274	2.74
10	305	3.05
50	1524*	15.24*
100	3048*	30.48*

1 yard = .9144* meters
1 rod = 5.0292* meters
1 mile = 1.6 kilometers
1 nautical mile = 1.852* kilometers

Weights

ounces	grams
1	28.3
2	56.7
3	85
4	113
5	142
6	170
7	198
8	227
9	255
10	283
11	312
12	340
13	369
14	397
15	425
16	454

Formula (exact):
ounces × 28.349 523 125* = grams

pounds	kilograms
1	.45
2	.9
3	1.4
4	1.8
5	2.3
6	2.7
7	3.2
8	3.6
9	4.1
10	4.5

1 short ton (2000 lbs) = 907 kilograms (kg)
Formula (exact):
pounds × .453 592 37* = kilograms

Fluid Measure

(Milliliters [ml] and cubic centimeters [cc] are equivalent, but it is customary to use milliliters for liquids.)

1 cu in = 16.39 ml
1 fl oz = 29.6 ml
1 cup = 237 ml
1 pint = 473 ml
1 quart = 946 ml
 = .946 liters
1 gallon = 3785 ml
 = 3.785 liters
Formula (exact):
fluid ounces × 29.573 529 562 5*
 = milliliters

Volume

1 cu in = 16.39 cubic centimeters (cc)
1 cu ft = 28 316.7 cc
1 bushel = 35 239.1 cc
1 peck = 8 809.8 cc

Area

1 sq in = 6.45 sq cm
1 sq ft = 929 sq cm
 = .093 sq meters
1 sq yd = .84 sq meters
1 acre = 4 046.9 sq meters
 = .404 7 hectares
1 sq mile = 2 589 988 sq meters
 = 259 hectares
 = 2.589 9 sq kilometers

Miscellaneous

1 British thermal unit (Btu) (mean)
 = 1 055.9 joules
1 horsepower = 745.7 watts
 = .75 kilowatts
caliber (diameter of a firearm's bore in hundredths of an inch)
 = .254 millimeters (mm)

1 atmosphere pressure = 101 325* pascals (newtons per sq meter)
1 pound per square inch (psi) = 6 895 pascals
1 pound per square foot = 47.9 pascals
1 knot = 1.85 kilometers per hour
1 mile per hour = 1.6093 kilometers per hour